**Foreword by
*Dr Temple Grandin***

The

Parent's

Guide

to the

Medical

World of

A Physician
*Explains
Diagnosis,
Medications
&
Treatments*

Autism

Edward Aull, MD

Behavioral Pediatrician

The Parent's Guide to the Medical World of Autism: A Physician Explains Diagnosis, Medications & Treatments

All marketing and publishing rights guaranteed to and reserved by:

FUTURE HORIZONS INC.

721 W. Abram St.
Arlington, TX 76013
(800) 489-0727
(817) 277-0727
(817) 277-2270 (fax)
E-mail: *info@fhautism.com*
www.fhautism.com

ISBN: 978-1-935274-89-6

This book is dedicated to those patients and families who have enlightened me over the years to the panorama of autism spectrum disorders.

Acknowledgments

I wish to thank Pamela Aull, Martha DellaValle, Martha Faul, and Delise Webber for reviewing the book and adding helpful commentary.

Preface

This book was written with the intention of helping families and professionals understand the difficulties and nuances of using medications to treat patients with autism spectrum disorders. Hopefully, after reading this book, you will understand some of the difficulties with using medication, and you'll understand why certain responses to treatment may be acceptable and some not. I hope it will be especially helpful to you if you have previously given medication a try without good success and you would be willing to give it a second chance. I hope to explain why medications may have met with poor success and why it may be worthwhile to give them another trial.

Since the writing of this book, the 5th edition of the Diagnostic and Statistical Manual of Mental Disorders (DSM-5) has been finalized and published. Severe autism, moderate autism, high-functioning autism, Asperger's syndrome, and pervasive developmental disorders—not otherwise specified have been subsumed under autism spectrum disorder. The autism spectrum is then divided by severity levels, which are dependent on the level of support required for social communication and restricted, repetitive behaviors.

Throughout this book, however, I am going to continue to use the DSM-IV terminology. I believe the older terminology is easier to understand, and I believe it will continue to be used by both professionals and families. It should be noted, however, that some of the patients I have written about who have milder autism may no longer meet the DSM-5 criteria for an autism spectrum disorder. Instead, they will meet the criteria for social (pragmatic) communication disorder. However, I believe many patients who meet the criteria for social communication disorder will benefit from medication treatments that are used for patients with autism spectrum disorders.

Foreword

by Temple Grandin, PhD

This is the first book I have read in which a wise and highly experienced physician has discussed his use of medications with many different types of individuals on the autism spectrum. Medications, when they are used with a careful, conservative approach, can help many individuals. I began taking a low dose of an antidepressant in my early 30s, and it stopped my perpetual anxiety and panic attacks. During my 20s, my anxiety progressively worsened. My nervous system was on high alert and was vigilant for nonexistent dangers. I was like a vigilant antelope on the African plains, constantly on the lookout for lions. The constant stress was destroying me, and I was wracked with headaches and colitis. Within 3 days of taking an antidepressant, my pounding heart, sweaty palms, and colitis almost completely vanished. Antidepressants, when they are prescribed correctly, can work wonders for anxiety. However, it is important not to give too high a dose. A dose that is too high may cause a person who has a high level of anxiety to experience insomnia and agitation. They will feel like they drank 20 cups of coffee.

In 2010, I learned why I had been so anxious. A brain scan conducted by Jason Cooperrider at the University of Utah showed that my amygdala in my brain was three times larger than normal. The amygdala is the brain's fear center. My nervous system had been operating in a constant state of fear. I have been taking 50 mg a day of desipramine for 35 years now. Since I am stable, I think the best thing to do is keep taking it.

Autism is highly variable—some individuals with autism have severe anxiety problems, and others do not. Several of my friends who are not autistic work in design, and they take a low dose of fluoxetine (trade name Prozac) to control their own anxiety and keep them from returning to an addiction to drugs and alcohol. There seems to be a link between anxiety and the artistic or mathematic mind. It appears that people on the autism spectrum who are good at art or math tend to have more anxiety than more verbal, word-based thinkers do, and these folks also often love history.

I do not have scientific evidence for this, but I have had conversations with folks at many autism meetings to support this observation.

The Dr Aull Diagnostic Continuum

Dr Aull has come up with an autism continuum that does not follow the *Diagnostic and Statistical Manual of Mental Disorders* diagnostic criteria. It is based on his many years of clinical practice. He discusses low-, moderate-, and high-functioning autism and low-, moderate-, and high-functioning Asperger's syndrome. It is best to view this as a continuum that ranges from the mildest autism traits to more severe cases. Dr Aull created his own autism continuum because it helped him prescribe the right medications. When you read this book, it is best to look at the different cases he presents and see which ones are most similar to your child or student.

This book is essential reading for every parent who has a child on the spectrum who is either taking medication or considering the use of medication. When I read over the patient examples he uses to illustrate the different "levels" of autism, most of the cases he presents seem to be on the moderate- to high-functioning end of the spectrum. He cited relatively few cases on the most severe end. This would include older individuals who are nonverbal and may have other serious conditions, such as epilepsy. This book provides very little discussion of anticonvulsant mood stabilizer drugs, which are often useful for anger attacks that "come out of the blue," with no stressful event preceding them. This is another indicator that the book may be most helpful for individuals who are either verbal or partially verbal.

A physician in Canada named Joe Huggins has worked with the most severe nonverbal clients who have been kicked out of many programs, owing to severe meltdowns. In this population, he found it was often best to avoid using antidepressant medications, and he used anticonvulsants instead, along with atypical antipsychotic medications and the beta-blocker propranolol, which is a blood pressure medication.

Tips for Using Medication

Here are some of the salient points I talk about when I speak to folks about starting medications:

1. A medication should have an obvious beneficial effect. When I began taking antidepressants, it was like, "Wow!" I'm a believer in biochemistry. The use of powerful antipsychotics, such as risperidone (Risperdal) or aripiprazole (Abilify), as sleep aids or to make a child a tiny bit less hyper is a bad idea, owing to the severe side effects. If the drug makes it possible to engage in more normal activities, however, then it can be worth the risk.

2. Try one thing at a time. Do not start a drug at the same time you start a new school or a special diet. Space them out by a few weeks, so you can see what works.

3. Do not increase the dose or add another medication every time there is a meltdown or a problem. Medication is only one tool in the toolbox for behavior problems. In most cases, one to three medications is usually sufficient to treat anxiety, depression, aggression, irritability, or an inability

to stay on task. There are, of course, some exceptions, but this is a good, general rule.

4. Be careful when changing brands of generics. This is especially important with time-release products. Dosages may have to be changed when the drug is obtained from a different vendor.

5. Too many powerful medications are being given to very young children who are younger than 6 years. A good basic principle is to be more conservative with medications in very young children.

Glossary of Terms

Abstraction: Considering something in general terms, apart from concrete realities.

ADHD: Attention-deficit/hyperactivity disorder, characterized by impulsivity, inattention, and, sometimes, physical hyperactivity.

Asperger's syndrome: High-functioning autism, with no significant language delay and no significant cognitive delay.

Augmentation: To enlarge in extent or strength.

Autism spectrum disorders: A term applied to patients who exhibit *(a)* difficulties with social issues and language and *(b)* repetitive behaviors. The spectrum generally includes autism, Asperger's syndrome, and pervasive developmental disorder—not otherwise specified (PDD-NOS).

Cognitive behavioral therapy: Psychotherapy that emphasizes the correction of distorted thinking associated with faulty self-perception or unrealistic expectations.

Co-morbid: Occurring at the same time, with a higher frequency than chance.

Dystonia: Involuntary muscle spasms that cause twisting of the body.

Echolalia: Immediate and uncontrollable repetition of words spoken by another person.

Impetus: Driving force.

Meltdown: A significant temper tantrum, usually precipitated by a transition or a denial.

Oppositional defiant disorder: A condition characterized by breaking rules and arguing with adults, parents, and peers.

Osmotic release: The movement of fluid across a semipermeable membrane within the drug capsule; causes a slow release of medication from the capsule.

Paradigm: An example that serves as a model.

Pedantic: An excessive or inappropriate display of learning.

PDD-NOS: Pervasive developmental disorder— not otherwise specified; an autism spectrum disorder with mild symptoms that does not meet the criteria for autism or Asperger's syndrome.

Reciprocal: Given or felt by each other.

Regression: Reversion to an earlier or less advanced state.

Salient: Most obvious or conspicuous.

SSRI: Selective serotonin reuptake inhibitor; a type of medication that functions via this method.

Static condition: Stable; not improving or worsening.

Stereotypies: Repetitive movements, such as hand flapping, which seem to have little purpose or function to others.

Introduction

I am a physician who specializes in behavioral pediatrics. I have been treating patients with autism spectrum disorders for more than 30 years. Some patients are mildly affected, and some severely affected. Most patients meet the criteria for a diagnosis on the autism spectrum somewhere between the two extremes. My patients have spanned the ages of 1 to 40 years. I wrote this book with the hopes of educating families who have a family member or members with an autism spectrum disorder and are involved in making decisions in their best interest.

I feel it would be helpful to families to have the information I've gathered on my understanding about why medication may improve symptoms. I also believe it is important for them to understand what the effects and side effects of medications are in patients with autism spectrum disorders. I am not the only physician who treats patients in the manner that will be described in this book. At meetings, I have found other physicians who seem to follow similar guidelines for treatment.

However, I have met with many families who had previously given medications a trial, did not obtain satisfactory results, and subsequently decided that medication wouldn't work for that particular patient. In my experience, the poor results may have been a result of less than ideal medication management by the treating physician. This does not mean that the physician was of poor quality; it means that his or her knowledge of autism and the medications used to treat autism was less than ideal.

Indeed, even at an incidence rate of 1 in 100, each physician is going to encounter some patients with an autism spectrum disorder, but he or she isn't going to treat enough patients with autism spectrum disorders to be highly capable when it comes to managing the subtle nuances of treatment.

My intention with this book is to explain my concepts about the use of medication to treat autism spectrum disorders, why medications might cause an adverse outcome, and what might be done to improve a patient's results.

I am a pediatrician with a behavioral practice that is limited to the treatment of attention-deficit/hyperactivity disorder (ADHD), autism, Asperger's syndrome, and their co-morbidities in patients ranging from young preschoolers to young adults.

I attended Indiana University for my undergraduate degree and subsequently attended Indiana University Medical School, where I graduated in 1969 with a Doctor of Medicine degree. I completed a residency in pediatrics at Riley Children's Hospital, which is part of the Indiana University medical school complex of hospitals. I was chief resident of pediatrics during my final year.

For my pediatric residency, I had a very special mentor in Dr Morris Green, the head of the pediatric residency program at Riley Hospital. He was also a pioneer in behavioral pediatrics and coauthored one of the first books on pediatric behavioral disorders. Dr Green was a unique and qualified physician, who would infuse the concepts of normal and abnormal behaviors into daily clinical experience. I often saw cases presented to him that had been worked up by a competent medical student or pediatric resident. Dr Green was very good at taking in the clinical information, asking one or two more questions of the patient or the patient's family, and coming up with a diagnosis that may not have even been considered. Dr Green greatly influenced my decision to be a physician who treats behavioral issues in children, adolescents, and young adults.

My first encounter with a patient who had autism was during my residency in pediatrics. He was an 8-year-old boy who was supposed to return to the Riley Hospital outpatient clinic twice a year because of a seizure disorder. Every year, his mother brought him in to the clinic. Each year he was attended to dutifully, usually by a physician doing his or her residency training, who likely hadn't seen him previously, and his medications would be refilled. At that time, Riley Hospital was the only children's hospital in Indiana.

On the day I met this boy, he was standing by the window, grunting and pointing at something in the parking lot. As I reviewed his chart, I noted that during previous visits, one or two physicians had recorded the fact that this child was nonverbal, but they had not scheduled him for an evaluation to assess his lack of language. I told the patient's mother that I thought her son had an autism spectrum disorder.

I then advised her that there was a neurologist on campus who treated children with autism, and

I scheduled an appointment for the patient to see her. However, on the day of his appointment, he was unable to get to the doctor's office because of snow and the distance he and his family had to travel. When the autism clinic personnel reviewed this boy's chart, they believed he only had a seizure disorder and refused to reschedule him.

Fortunately, I was able to intercede and get a new appointment scheduled. The family was able to attend the new appointment and get help for their child. At the time of my residency, there were not a lot of medications being used to treat patients with autism spectrum disorders. But, when I met with this 8-year-old boy, I believed it was an injustice to the family that no one had addressed an almost certain diagnosis of autism.

Then and now, I believe that whether a family decides to use or not use medications, knowledge of the disorder is important and helpful. When a family can understand why a certain behavior occurs, they are better able to deal with it.

I started out in a general pediatric practice in the early 1970s, and, very early in that practice, I began treating patients with ADHD. By the early 1980s, I was recognizing that some of the patients with symptoms of ADHD had milder forms of autism spectrum disorders. With the recognition of an amended diagnosis, I began prescribing medications for patients with autism spectrum disorders and the ADHD that went with them. I did not believe that I was an expert in autism spectrum disorders at that time, but I seemed to know more than most other physicians I encountered. I began reading and attending medical conferences concerning autism. Over the years, my patients and their families have taught me extensively about both the obvious and subtle aspects of autism spectrum disorders and the treatment of these disorders with medications.

It was early in my general pediatric practice when I met with my second patient with autism. The patient was a 9-year-old boy who had almost no language and was experiencing frequent "meltdowns." At that time, I told the patient's mother that his diagnosis was autism and that medical care had little to offer to help him. I sent them for counseling. I believe I was correct at that time, but I now devote a large portion of my practice to using medications to treat children and young adults with autism spectrum disorders, in an attempt to minimize their difficulties.

I have come to realize that my training in normative behavior did not begin in medical school, but began instead during my childhood.

I have eight brothers and sisters. I am not saying that they are all "normal"—whatever that is—but, through many years of interactions with my siblings and their friends, I incurred a lot of unsolicited instruction in child and adolescent behavior.

I believe, and there is scientific evidence to support this concept, that ADHD and autism are genetic neurodevelopmental differences that have been around for generations. Over time, society and its rules have changed, which may have made these disorders more evident. Those societal changes may make it appear that there is an increased incidence of both ADHD and autism spectrum disorders.

When I was a child and I came home from school, I was simply sent out to play. Back then, there was no designated "play group" where your mother took you. You found your own group. I was a skinny kid, and not very athletic. There were, however, a lot more kids in the neighborhood to play with than there are now. The families who lived nearby were generally larger, and the children did not have electronic games to play that might keep them indoors. At the baseball games held in the vacant lot in our neighborhood, I was always the last one picked, but everyone always got picked, and there were no adults around to ensure that happened. I am not certain that things would go the same way today for my patients with autism spectrum disorders. I believe that today, many of my patients would be told by their peers to go elsewhere, rather than be included.

Children nowadays have significantly more information to learn than a child did in 1980. It can be as much as 30% more. Therefore, any learning difficulties that a student might have are more likely to interfere with his or her school performance. The increased academic load is likely to expose academic difficulties in students who have both ADHD and autism spectrum disorders.

I feel I was brought into the treatment of autism spectrum disorders in a reverse manner. My forte in my early years of practice was the treatment of ADHD. As I began to reevaluate patients who were not responding to their medications as well as I thought they should, I began to recognize that in some, the diagnosis of ADHD was incomplete. It was not really incorrect—they did indeed have ADHD—but it was not their entire issue. I began to see that these patients—especially those in whom the ADHD medication would be helpful for a while (perhaps 2 or 3 months) and then quit working—were more likely to have high-functioning autism or bipolar disorder, and their medications therefore needed to be altered. This unusual effect, where an ADHD medication works only for a short while, is consistent enough that, when seen, it can be used to help assign a diagnosis of an autism spectrum disorder.

In 1996, I made the decision to quit practicing general pediatrics. Since that time, I only treat patients with autism spectrum disorders, ADHD, and the co-morbidities that occur with those disorders. Most of my patients are from a wide area of Indiana and the surrounding states, but, over the years, I have had a few who have come from a greater distance.

I believe that my 24 years of general pediatrics has been invaluable in teaching me about normative behavior for each age level, as well as where the limits of that normal behavior might be. There will always be discussions among parents and professionals about what behavior is "normal." The demarcation lines of normal behavior are fuzzy, rather than sharp. For example, a short attention span is normal and accepted in a 1- or 2-year-old, but not in a third-grade student.

When I treat a patient, especially one with an autism spectrum disorder, my goal is to try to modify behaviors, so that most individuals the patient encounters do not know the patient has any problems at all. This may end up being impossible to accomplish, but it is always a goal.

Several years ago, I was treating a 14-year-old girl who had Asperger's syndrome. After she started taking her medication, she skipped out on a class in high school. I was pleased. Her mother wasn't. My understanding of that situation was that the medication had lowered her anxiety level about getting into trouble, and she had skipped class to be with her friends—which many of her normally developing classmates might also have done. Her mother was upset that she violated the school rules, which her daughter had been extremely reluctant to do in the past. Her behavior had broken a school rule, but, it meant she had tried a social behavior that was normal for her age.

Many patients with Asperger's syndrome have difficulty making and keeping friends, which is partially due to their rigidity about rules and anxiety about breaking those rules. If the patient can be more adaptable about rules, and not so black and white in his thinking, he may be included in social situations more often.

If a family is in a store and has a child with a problem that is obvious to others, such as

Down syndrome, and the child misbehaves, most people feel sorry for the parents. But, if you have a child that appears outwardly normal, as most children with an autism spectrum disorder do, when he misbehaves, other people's behavior indicates they think he has bad or incapable parents. I had one mother who was so upset about the glares she got from others when she was out in public with her son that she had a t-shirt made that read, "He has autism—that's why he's acting this way!"

A major factor in improving behavior, especially with medication, is to assign the correct or nearly correct diagnosis. Some diagnoses cannot be assigned at the first visit to the doctor and are evolving diagnoses. As I stated previously, an individual's response to medication may be helpful in leading to the correct diagnosis or diagnoses. I believe that if the response to medication does not improve the patient's symptoms the way it is expected to, it is usually one of the three "D"s: wrong *drug*, wrong *dose*, or wrong *diagnosis*.

In this book, I am going to try to inform you about the different types of autism. I will include some of the causes of behavioral, social, and learning difficulties that patients with an autism spectrum disorder experience, the medications

I might use for each one, and why. I will discuss what types of symptoms may not be susceptible to medications, at least at this time. Further, I will discuss what may be causing difficulties at school and what can be assessed to improve the likelihood of eventual employment.

As I discuss patients, I will use the pronoun "he" most often, rather than repeatedly using "he" and "she." This will simplify your reading. It is currently believed that autism spectrum disorders occur at an incidence rate of four times higher in males versus females. This ratio may come closer to three to one or two to one in the future, as milder cases are diagnosed, but for now, autism spectrum disorders are much more commonly diagnosed in males.

Diagnosis of Autism Spectrum Disorders

The *Diagnostic and Statistical Manual of Mental Disorders* (DSM) is a book authored by the American Psychiatric Association, which contains discussions of the symptoms that are used to define a certain psychiatric diagnosis. The latest edition is the DSM-5, published in 2013.

Within the DSM-IV there is a chapter on "pervasive developmental disorders." Autism and Asperger's syndrome are found in this section. Also included in this section are Rett syndrome, childhood disintegrative disorder, and pervasive developmental disorder—not otherwise specified

(PDD-NOS). This last category is a diagnosis used to describe a patient who has autistic characteristics but does not meet the full criteria for classic autism or Asperger's syndrome. A major problem, even between professionals in the field, is deciding what the limits of each of these categories are. There may be quite a variation in the diagnoses assigned to patients among different clinical centers, particularly with regard to the diagnoses of Asperger's syndrome and PDD-NOS.

There is good evidence to show that children can move higher along the autism spectrum— that is, display milder symptoms—as they age and mature. An example that might cause diagnostic difficulty would be a child who is finally developing reciprocal language at 4 years of age. He meets the criteria for a language delay and therefore would not meet the strict criteria for Asperger's syndrome. However, it is predictable that if language progresses enough, by 8 or 9 years of age, he will communicate like a child with Asperger's syndrome and respond to treatment as would a child with this disorder. At 8 or 9 years of age, I am more likely to consider this child to have a diagnosis of Asperger's syndrome rather than PDD-NOS, but that is not the view across all professional disciplines.

As noted in the preface, Asperger's syndrome, PDD-NOS, and high-functioning autism have been subsumed into autism spectrum disorders in the DSM-5. Personally, I do believe that autism, Asperger's syndrome, and PDD-NOS are diagnoses that occur along a continuum, from severe to mild. I believe when the diagnosis is broken down into different categories of severity, it is easier for families to find information that seems to closely relate to the issues they encounter. It may also create difficulties with reaching significant conclusions in scientific studies if a wide group of patients with autism spectrum disorders is studied, rather than a group of patients with a narrower spectrum of symptoms, such as Asperger's syndrome.

In general professional use, classic autism is usually defined as severe, moderate, or high functioning. There are no official criteria for each of these levels, but most professionals who deal with autism easily relate to discussions that include these divisions. They are based on intelligence level, language abilities, social capabilities, and other symptoms related to autism, such as self-injury and aggression.

I divide Asperger's syndrome into five categories, which I will go into later, because it seems to help me be able to predict issues and response to treatments. As with almost every difference, the milder the disorder, the easier it is to improve.

Because of its inherent mild nature, the category of PDD-NOS is not divided. I am much more likely to assign a diagnosis of a higher-functioning form of Asperger's syndrome than PDD-NOS. I have found that many professionals are more likely to assign the PDD-NOS diagnosis. This variation between diagnoses of PDD-NOS and Asperger's syndrome is quite common. I attended a conference at Johns Hopkins Medical School a few years ago, where the lecturer stated, "A diagnosis of PDD means that the physician didn't decide."

Childhood disintegrative disorder is very rare. It is characterized by significant and permanent loss of language and social skills. Its cause is unknown at this time, but it is clearly not typical of other autism spectrum disorders. Although regression, especially in language and social skills, does occur with autism spectrum disorders, it is not as severe and not as permanent as that seen in childhood disintegrative disorder. There has been some recent evidence that children with autism who experience regression in speech and social skills may have a poorer long-term outcome than those who developed language at a later age but did not experience a regression in language and social skills. However, the concept of a poorer prognosis with regression is yet to be proven, so do not be disheartened if your family member belongs to this category.

I will continue to use the term *Asperger's syndrome*, even though it has been discontinued in the DSM-5. When I talk with families, I believe it is easier to explain the diagnosis of Asperger's syndrome than the broader diagnosis of an autism spectrum disorder. I find it is easier for families to find information that seems to apply to their child if I distinguish between autism and Asperger's syndrome. I never state nor imply to a family that a child with Asperger's syndrome is not on the autistic spectrum. Understanding the various levels of autism spectrum disorders is helpful to families when they are sorting through the wealth of available information.

There are many clues I search for during the initial evaluation, which may help me decide if a patient has an autism spectrum disorder. Some clues are just observations. A patient who does not make conversation or eye contact, who walks about the room on his tiptoes, does not present a diagnostic dilemma.

I evaluated the child of a family who had im-migrated to the United States from eastern Africa.

When I noted the child was up on his toes a lot and asked if that was common for him, the mother questioned if that had anything to do with autism. I replied affirmatively, and she stated, "There are a lot of children in Africa who are on their tiptoes and don't talk." Almost certainly, there are a lot of children and adults with an autism spectrum disorder throughout the world that have not received a diagnosis or treatment.

During an evaluation, I look for a history of anxiety, as well as social, language, and sensory issues. For example, I met with a 17-year-old male a few years ago for an initial evaluation. There were two clues for me as to the diagnosis, upon just entering the exam room. For one, he was not upset enough about being brought in by his parents to see me. Number two, his clothing was folded neatly on the exam table, which is unusual for a 17-year-old male.

During the interview, I asked him if he had a steady girlfriend, and he replied that he did. I asked him how long he had had this girlfriend, and he replied, "Three months and four days." Most normally developing males his age have little idea how long they have had a girlfriend, especially to the day. I later asked if he and his girlfriend of three months and four days kissed and made out, and he replied, "No, she is kind of shy." Most relationships at 17 years of age involve kissing a week or two into the relationship.

I typically ask parents about how the child played with toys as a toddler. I'm looking for a lack of imaginative play. This may mean that a child who has plastic building blocks only builds the model that is on the cover of the box. In a child with an autism spectrum disorder, playing with dolls or action figures may be limited to only certain structured routines or scripted scenes.

There may be a history of having difficulty with sharing toys with a friend or relative who is visiting, even if the toy is not fragile. Patients with autism spectrum disorders often know exactly how many toy cars or trading cards they have and may become quite upset if even one is missing. It is not rare to hear that there must be a certain number of stuffed animals or a certain arrangement of those stuffed animals on the bed for the patient to be able to go to sleep at night. Many families are unaware that this behavior may be a part of an autism spectrum disorder. They are looking for more severe manifestations of the disorder.

I had a patient whose appointment was set up to be on his family's way out of town for spring break. When they left home, they traveled 1½ hours north, to my office. They were going to Chicago, which is about 3½ hours north of my office. On the way to my clinic, it was discovered that my patient had brought his favorite games for the Nintendo DS, but his sister had forgotten the Nintendo game unit. The family was going to stop and purchase a new game unit, because they knew that the patient would obsess about the lack of the game system and ruin the trip for the rest of the family. I believe anxiety drives this need for the patient to have outcomes the way he had planned.

I ask if a child took toys apart or if he was likely to leave them outside. Many patients with autism spectrum disorders are overly careful with their toys. Others seem to care less. Some do not play with toys at all but may watch videos repeatedly for long periods of time. I am looking for a history of a patient viewing the same video over and over again or perhaps going to a particular part of a video and replaying that part again and again. This behavior is typical in patients with an autism spectrum disorder, particularly at a young age. There tends to be improvement in this obsessive viewing as they grow older. A typical example of more significant forms of autism is a patient who carries a toy around for a major part of the day but does not really play with it. He just has to have a toy in his hand. It may have to be a certain toy, but, often, it is just something that fits his hand well. If it is a small car, he may spin the wheels but not really play with it, as if it were a vehicle that he is driving.

My favorite question for young children is, "Do you know a story about a little girl who went to her grandmother's house and found that her grandmother had been eaten by a wolf?" They usually respond affirmatively, and I ask, "What color was her cape?" They usually respond with "Red," and I ask, "Why did she wear it?" The typical response is that they do not know, but sometimes, they state that her grandmother had made it for her. I suggest, perhaps she couldn't find her coat and it was cool outside, so she wore her hooded red cape. The typical response from a patient with Asperger's syndrome is, "It doesn't say that!" Patients with an autism spectrum disorder are reluctant to add or infer information that is not presented in the text.

I ask about anxieties, such as worrying about storms or robbers. Several of my patients have their own weather radios in their rooms, and their anxiety rises with severe weather alerts or warnings. It might be appropriate to worry about tornadoes or hurricanes, but, often, the patient's concern is easily seen as being excessive. Concern about robbers may lead to excessive checking of locks and windows and the inability to fall asleep alone.

Are there clothing issues? Are there clothes or types of clothing that the patient will not wear because of the way they feel, rather than the way they look? This is another issue that tends to lessen with age, so I have to ask about these symptoms in a child's younger years. Some will still have issues, even as a teen or young adult. Common remarks are, "He wouldn't wear blue jeans, because they were too stiff." "He wouldn't wear a belt, because of the pressure on his stomach." "He wouldn't wear shirts with embroidery on them, or shirts with buttons." Turtlenecks are frequently avoided, but one may see that as an issue even in patients who are typically developing.

A question I have for every family is, "Does he have any problem with his socks?" If a patient has trouble with the seam in the toe of his sock, if he frequently complains about how it feels or he constantly adjusts the seam to get it just right, I highly suspect a diagnosis of an autism spectrum disorder. On occasion, I will hear that the patient doesn't have trouble with his socks, but his sibling does. If the sibling has trouble with the seam in the toe of his sock, it may be an indication that that child has autistic symptoms. It would then be more likely that an autism spectrum disorder is the correct diagnosis in the patient I'm evaluating, because the disorder is seen with a greater frequency in siblings. I had one patient's mother who had purchased 50 pairs of socks to find seven pairs that her son would wear. Some of my patients feel they can tell if they are wearing a left or a right tube sock.

It is important to inquire about personal hygiene issues. Many patients with autism spectrum disorders will bathe infrequently, unless his parents require otherwise. A common inquiry of mine is, "If you sent him to take a shower and there was no soap or shampoo, what would he do?" A typically developing teen or preteen would start yelling at his mother to bring some supplies, but most of my patients with an autism spectrum disorder would simply shower without soap or shampoo. The patient with an autism spectrum disorder sees no problem with having taken a shower without soap.

I always ask what TV shows the patient watches. I am especially looking for the patient who is watching shows that are not age appropriate. Watching "Sponge Bob" or "Barney" as a teenager is not appropriate and can be a social problem. It is a social problem especially if a teen tries to bring it up in conversation in the middle-school cafeteria. I did have one patient, however, who acquired some appreciation from his peers because he could deliver the school announcements over the public address system by exactly mimicking the voice of "Sponge Bob."

Some patients essentially watch only nonfiction programming, such as the History Channel or Discovery Channel. They see no need to watch or read something that someone simply made up in their head. In my patients with autism spectrum disorders, watching the Cartoon Network is common. Some watch the Weather Channel a lot. Animal Planet is also a common favorite.

Sometimes, there are outside factors that help me assign a diagnosis. I saw a new patient recently who was in the seventh grade and had received a diagnosis of attention-deficit/hyperactivity disorder (ADHD), but her medication wasn't working very well. Her conversation was rather glib, but it was also too matter-of-fact or pedantic at times. There were some other clues to suggest to me that she might have Asperger's syndrome, but an interesting thing happened when I brought up the possibility of that diagnosis. Tears came to her mother's eyes, and I asked if she knew what Asperger's syndrome was. "No," she said, she had never heard of it before that day, but while she was waiting for me to come to the exam room, she had read a book that was sitting on the counter in the room. The book is by Kathy Hoopman and is titled, *All Cats Have Asperger's Syndrome.* She had picked up the book to read because her family loves cats. As she read the book, which has cute cat photos and is instructive about the symptoms of Asperger's syndrome, she recognized that it was describing symptoms she had seen in her daughter.

There are standardized tests to evaluate both autism and Asperger's syndrome. It is important to be aware that they are typically set up to avoid overdiagnosis and therefore may pass over, or fail to help identify, a patient with mild symptoms. Most patients who receive a diagnosis according to the results of these standardized tests are fairly easily diagnosed clinically by a professional who is experienced in evaluating patients with autism spectrum disorders. The tests may be helpful as secondary evaluations to solidify the diagnosis with the family or school.

In my office, the initial evaluation always includes a physical exam. Typically, there is not a lot to find in a physical exam, because most patients with an autism spectrum disorder appear "normal." There may be some neurologic "soft signs" that are seen in association with autism, but they are not diagnostic. One "soft sign" is clumsiness or fine-motor difficulty. Finding increased deep-tendon reflexes with mildly sustained clonus is another. *Clonus* is a finding where the forefoot is held in slight upward tension, while the Achilles tendon is tapped with the reflex hammer. If clonus is found, the forefoot continues to "beat" for a few beats without tapping the tendon again. It is not rare to find clonus in a child with an autism spectrum disorder, but it is not diagnostic.

It is important to look for physical findings that might suggest a genetic syndrome. Mild genetic syndromes often seem to have autistic features. One may find physical features typical of fetal alcohol effect (physical features seen in a child that developed during pregnancy when the mother was drinking too much alcohol), which has symptoms similar to autism. Short stature is commonly seen in mild genetic syndromes. During the exam, the professional should be evaluating eye contact and reciprocal conversation. Lack of adequate eye contact or very fleeting, nonsustained eye contact is often seen in patients with an autism spectrum disorder and not infrequently in the relatives who have come with them to the appointment.

On occasion, during the examination, one will see excessive anxiety exhibited as the patient cowers away from the reflex hammer, blood pressure cuff, or otoscope. Any kind of excessive fear or anxiety may be suggestive of an autism spectrum disorder. During one consultation with a 16-month-old boy, the child's mother begged me to not look in her son's ears. She said it would take 3 days to calm the child down if I did. The child screamed in pain when I laid the stethoscope on his chest. When the child was crawling on the floor, he was fine, unless the mother or I began laughing, and then he would start crying as if he had been physically struck. This child could not tolerate even mild sensory input in his environment.

Dr Morris Green was concerned that families did not appreciate the value of gathering a good patient history and performing a physical exam. Families seem to have more faith in blood tests and x-rays. In autism spectrum disorders, the history is often the most revealing, because the physical exam findings may be normal or nearly normal. In the future, there may be brain studies and genetic studies that are helpful in assigning an autism spectrum diagnosis, but, at this time, they are of limited value. To date, the differences that have been detected are mild enough that they only show a significant difference in group studies, where 50 patients with autism might be compared with 50 patients who have typical development.

A thorough patient history and physical exam require time. I met with a preteen male for his initial evaluation, which was about his inattention. About 40 minutes into the evaluation, while sitting on the exam table, he began sobbing. He was highly fearful about a broken downspout on his house that would knock on the wall in his room at night. Although his parents may have been aware of some of his anxiety issues, they were as surprised as I was at the severity he exhibited during the exam. During a short appointment, he never would have exhibited this important information. A thorough evaluation may require more than one appointment.

In summary, a thorough patient history and physical exam are the best tests to confirm a diagnosis of an autism spectrum disorder. The diagnosis may be suspected but not confirmed until a later time. Simply the knowledge that an autism spectrum disorder may be a possibility may help the family to understand certain behaviors and aid the family in helping both the patient and the professional who is overseeing treatment.

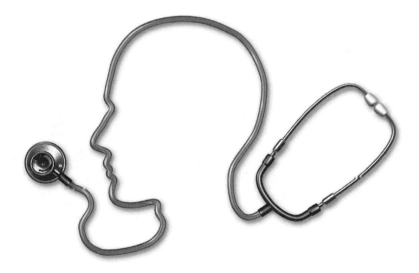

Chapter 2

Causes of
Autism

At the time of this writing, the cause of autism spectrum disorders is unknown. It is not even known if they have a single cause. It is known that there has been an increase in the incidence of the diagnosis of autism spectrum disorders, although the increase appears to be mostly related to a change in diagnostic definitions and some movement of patient diagnoses from a mental retardation diagnosis to an autism spectrum diagnosis.

Prior to 1990, the incidence of autism was thought to be four in 10,000 children. A study by the National Institute of Mental Health in 1990 yielded an incidence of 12.3 in 10,000 children. It is to be noted that 70% of patients in that study were mentally retarded, defined as having an IQ of 70 or less. I treat a lot of patients with a normal intelligence level and also many patients with a high level of intelligence who have an autism spectrum diagnosis. Therefore, I know that in the 1990 study, a lot of mild cases of autism spectrum disorders were missed.

In the year 2000, there was an article in the magazine *Science* that suggested that the nearly tenfold increase in the diagnoses of autistic spectrum disorders at that time was primarily related to the better recognition of the more common, milder forms of the disorder. It has been found that there has not been any real increase in the incidence of the diagnosis of severe and moderate autism.

There are multiple scientific studies to show that the incidence of autism is much more common in identical twins (monozygotic) than in nonidentical twins (dizygotic). This finding is highly supportive of a genetic factor in autism spectrum disorders. In fact, most of the medical studies support a primarily genetic issue. Genetics is not the only issue. It has been shown that the more prematurely an infant is born, the higher the incidence of an autism spectrum disorder. Also, infants who were born when the mother had been given thalidomide, a drug no longer used during pregnancy, have a more than 20% incidence of autism. There have been studies in which increased incidence pointed to advancing paternal age, less than 2 years between the birth of siblings, and the use of in vitro fertilization. Why any of these factors might be important to the cause of autism spectrum disorders is still unknown.

Brain studies in patients with autism spectrum disorders—mostly magnetic resonance (MR) imaging and autopsy studies—show small differences in the cerebellum, the wiring from the cerebellum to the upper brain, the amygdala, the prefrontal cortex, and the minicolumns in the outer cortex of the brain. The cerebellum is related to language, balance, and time considerations, such as "on top of" and "behind." Parts of the prefrontal cortex have to do with attention and focus. The amygdala is a crossover network area and helps with being able to ignore unimportant stimuli.

There are some very important concepts to be learned from these studies. Number one, the difference is already there. Most patients are not going to get worse, and, in fact, there will be improvement over time, even if nothing is done. Some children do lose language and social interest. I cannot explain why this happens, although I suspect it has a genetic basis. Most patients do not regress, except perhaps in a situation of high anxiety. Number two, for any of these studies to be correct, the difference had to occur prior to 28 weeks' gestation of pregnancy. The changes did not occur at birth, nor when the child fell off the changing table, nor with an infection. There has been a lot of concern that immunizations might have an effect on autism, but studies such as these would not support that concept.

In my experience, most cases are genetic in origin. If you sat in my office and met with families day after day, you would see that genes appear to be a major factor. If I diagnose Asperger's syndrome, the most likely occupation for the patient's father is engineering. But, it is also common to see occupations such as computer geek, lab researcher, accountant, and architect. These occupations often represent very bright people, indeed, but they may be very "black and white" in the way they see things. The occupations of a father, brother, or grandfather may be helpful information to have when assigning a diagnosis. I had a patient's father tell me that his father, who had a PhD in physics, would just walk away from a conversation without speaking a word to the other person, if he felt the conversation was not educating him in some manner.

I don't often see signs of Asperger's syndrome in a child's mother, but I do often see depression, anxiety disorders, and obsessive-compulsive disorder in mothers. I look for the possibility of Asperger's syndrome issues in a mother's father, brother, or uncle. I was explaining to a new patient's mother that there would always be issues with her son about things like failing to plan, failing to understand that he fails to understand, and failing to understand that what he does tonight will have an effect at a later time. She exclaimed, "That's my brother!" Her brother was an architect who was clueless as to why others got upset when he didn't have projects finished in a timely manner. I typically see that patients tend to get their autism spectrum disorder from both sides of the family tree, not just one. Many years ago, I met with a family in which the mother had received a diagnosis of Asperger's syndrome. Her husband, who was a math professor at a college, was clearly a person with Asperger's syndrome. Their son had full-blown moderate autism.

I recall a new patient who had an initial evaluation scheduled, but my office was able to move the appointment up to an earlier day, owing to a cancellation. The mother, a physician, could not come on the new appointment day, but the child's father could, and he did a good job of relating symptoms and issues. When the mother came in for the first follow-up visit, I started to explain Asperger's syndrome to her. She interrupted me and said, "You don't have to explain it to me—my family is full of very smart men who never married." A history of very smart men who never married or married at a late age is a good hint of possible autism spectrum disorders in the family.

Several of my patients' parents are physicians, whom I believe have Asperger's syndrome. One parent is a surgeon. His wife, who works with him in the office, relates that he is a very caring physician, and his patients love him. His problem is that he cannot keep a partner. Things always have to be done his way, and his way only. Several of my patients' fathers are airplane mechanics. I believe it to be an asset to employ someone who is obsessive about his work, doing repairs on an airplane where mistakes may be disastrous.

Genetics play a role in almost everything I see, including ADHD, bipolar disorders, anxiety, and autism spectrum disorders. The adage about the apple not falling far from the tree is supported repeatedly in my practice. One patient's mother told a story about how her son's father left them when her son was just 2 weeks old. Her son has never seen him. He is 12 now, and he cuts his steak just like his father did.

I believe that research will eventually uncover the cause or causes of autism spectrum disorders. An important question for families that needs to be answered is, "What is the risk of my child having an autism spectrum disorder if I have a sibling on the spectrum?"

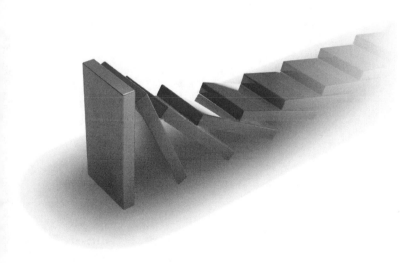

Chapter 3

Evaluations

My initial evaluation of a new patient takes about 1½ to 2 hours. As I stated previously, the evaluation includes a physical exam of the patient and a prolonged review of symptoms. When evaluating a patient for an autism spectrum disorder, the review will be especially focused on language development and usage, anxiety, attention and school performance, social abilities, and sensory issues. I ask the family and the child's teachers to fill out behavioral questionnaires, and I review those questionnaires. Any testing findings or evaluations from the past are reviewed. By the end of the initial evaluation, I have a working diagnosis. I also have possible reasons why the patient should start taking a certain medication. Or, I may have reasons why some medications should not be used with a particular patient.

I use the term "working diagnosis" if I believe the main issues affecting a patient are related to a diagnosis of ADHD or perhaps Asperger's syndrome. The difficulty is that even with a lengthy appointment, not all issues are brought to light at the first visit, and the diagnosis may need to be amended at a later time. Families do not always understand that a certain issue or behavior is important or relevant to being able to determine the patient's diagnosis. A typical conclusion at the end of an appointment would be the following: ADHD seems to be the primary diagnosis, but there are some bits and pieces of Asperger's syndrome, and there are some symptoms of anxiety.

I explain to families that it may take a while—1 to 2 years—to be completely certain of the diagnosis. They need to allow me about a year to get any medication treatment correct. I may get it correct prior to 1 year, but, if I do, it will come from a bit of educated guesswork. There is nothing about a patient's sex, size, or symptoms that tells me which medications will work the best or how much of a dose they will require.

It has been predicted that less than 30 years from now, a patient will simply have to undergo MR imaging for the physician to be able to determine the exact diagnosis, and a genetic blood test will let the physician know which medications will work the best. Until then, it is an educated guess as to what is causing the problem and what medication or medications will result in the most improvement in symptoms. I tell families, "Depending on which four of his seven symptoms I choose to focus on, I can diagnose ADHD, autism, anxiety disorder, bipolar disorder, depression, or even schizophrenia." Knowing which diagnosis is the most appropriate will be related to the training and experience of the professional who is treating the patient. And, of course, occasionally there are multiple diagnoses, although multiple diagnoses in one patient are less common in children and adolescents than in adults.

Autism spectrum disorders are not typically static conditions. A static disorder is one that is stable over time, with little or no improvement or worsening. In autism there is typically improvement over time, through the age of 30 or so, even if there is no treatment with medications. Therefore, ongoing reevaluation of symptoms and medications is needed. I believe the minimum follow-up time should be about every 3 to 4 months in children and adolescents who are stable, and perhaps a bit longer in stable adults. When things are not going well, patients are going to need to be evaluated more often, and that might mean every 1 to 2 weeks. Hospitalization for evaluation is not recommended, as it places the patient in an abnormal environment, which may greatly aggravate his anxiety. Also, hospitalizations are typically too brief to allow a patient to adjust to a new medication or dosage before being able to evaluate the effects of the medication properly.

Follow-up appointments at my office take approximately 30 minutes. Since parents do not always know what information I need to know to figure out what might need to be changed in the patient's treatment program, it is important that there is enough time for discussion. The family might tell me something that I consider very important with regard to the patient's treatment, but they had no idea it was significant or related to the medication. For example, a teenager who is frequently taking naps after school, when he has had an adequate amount of sleep the night before, is very likely experiencing a medication side effect, but, it could be another issue, such as depression or drug abuse. There are a few patients with autism spectrum disorders who appear to nap merely to avoid boredom.

Sometimes when you adjust the dosage of a medication, this adjustment may actually affect

the dosage levels of another medication or medications. The result of taking two medications may
cause a side effect, such as sleepiness, which
might not be seen in patients who take only one
of those medications at a particular dosage.

It is important for me to see the patient face to
face. I have some patients who travel quite a distance, who would like to do appointments over
the phone, but it has just not worked out well,
from my point of view, when it has been tried. It
is important for me to see how the patient inter-
acts with the family and with me. In the office, I
can assess his anxiety level, his pragmatics, and
his attention span. Unfortunately, I may also get
to see his aggression toward his parents or his
manipulation of his parents. I may observe clues
as to how stable the parents' marriage might be,
which could be causing stress for the patient.
Having children with difficulties can be hard on
a marriage. Marriage and behavioral counseling are often a part of treatment in the families I
work with.

I always talk to the patient during an appointment, often before I speak with the parents—
even if the patient doesn't have language. In a
study of follow-up appointments for ADHD, which
involved tracking good physicians, it was found

that in 40% of visits, the physician only spoke with the parents. I always try to include the patient when I evaluate him for medications and side effects. Occasionally, by speaking with the child, I can find out about issues that the family was not aware of.

One of the issues that comes up sometimes is that the patient is being bullied at school or on the school bus. Being bullied is very common in patients with autism spectrum disorders. Unfortunately, my patients are typically the recipients of bullying rather than the ones doing the bullying, but on occasion it goes the other way—particularly if the patient is big for his age or is older than most of his classmates.

I have also seen a few instances where my patient is a fifth or sixth grader, and I find out he is bullying a second grader. My observation has been that the milder the degree of an autism spectrum disorder, the more likely one is bullied. My more severely autistic patients, whose odd behaviors are obvious to everyone, are typically left alone, but the patients with milder Asperger's syndrome are frequently bullied, both physically and emotionally.

Other students or neighbors may not know the exact diagnosis of a patient, but they certainly know that they can set the child up to get into trouble, get mad, or cry. The patient may not know that his or her parents should be informed about these issues. A patient with an autism spectrum disorder may be unaware that the bullying is being done to him on purpose.

I have a patient, a freshman in high school, who was trying to "fit in" and grabbed a girl's breast in the school hallway on a dare. He was so "set up" that some of his classmates had the time to record the incident on their cell phones. My patient related to me, "I didn't want to be called a chicken." He is certainly smart enough to know that what he did was not socially appropriate and might get him in trouble. He did get in trouble. He got a 3-day suspension—but the girl who dared him was expelled! However, being bullied doesn't always have as reasonable an outcome as this case did. We have seen poor outcomes exposed by the media, with instances resulting in violence and suicides. Bullying continues to get a lot of attention in research, but, to date, no one has been able to clearly define the best therapies to be able to help the person being bullied, as well as the person doing the bullying.

At this time, most patients who have an autism spectrum disorder and consult either me or another physician who regularly treats autism spectrum disorders will end up taking one to four medications. Figuring out whether the issue presented is related to medication, maturation, growth, learning issues, and the like can rarely be done in a 5- to 7-minute appointment. However, studies do show that brief standardized question-naires are helpful to the professional in evaluat-ing a patient when the time available is limited.

Patients reach a stage around puberty that I fondly call the "A" stage. Is the issue being evaluat-ed related to ADHD, autism, anxiety, adolescence, or antisocial behavior? It takes time and a very skilled clinician to be able to sort out the cause or causes of the current, most impairing issue and what might be done to improve the situation.

Chapter

4

Autism

According

to the American Psychiatric Association, autism is a complex neurobehavioral syndrome that is behaviorally defined and qualitatively revealed through *(a)* disruption in the development of social skills, language, and communication skills and *(b)* the presence of restricted interests and/or stereotyped behaviors. Described in 1943 by Leo Kanner, classic autism describes patients with very limited reciprocal conversation, little or no social contacts, and little probability of living on one's own in a nonsheltered environment.

Clinically, classic autism is described as severe, moderate, or high functioning. Although this division is reasonably understood and useful in discussions among professionals and in studies, these separations of degree of functioning are not officially described categories, and their limits are blurred.

In a recent study, an IQ score of 80 and higher was used to differentiate high-functioning patients from those with moderate or severe autism. An IQ score of 80 and higher is not a standardized norm, but it does seem to me to be a reasonable level to be able to differentiate high-functioning autism from moderate autism. One problem is that autism, itself, may affect how a patient scores on an IQ test, often resulting in lower IQ scores and a lower designation of functioning.

Patients with severe autism tend to have little or no reciprocal language. This does not mean they have no words, and, commonly, they use some language to get their basic needs met. "Go home," "French fries," or "drink" might be typical examples of words used to get needs met. Patients in this category are more likely to *(a)* engage in self-injurious behavior, *(b)* display stereotypical behaviors, such as hand flapping, rocking, and watching rotating objects like ceiling fans and toy car wheels, and *(c)* have outbursts and display aggression when they become upset.

This group of patients is the most likely to receive a diagnosis of a significant mental handicap and the most likely to have seizures. It is really the outbursts and aggression in this group of patients that have resulted in obtaining U.S. Food and Drug Administration (FDA) approval for treatment of autism with two of the antipsychotic medications now on the market, aripiprazole (trade name Abilify) and risperidone (trade name Risperdal). These medications will be discussed later.

Patients with classic autism may be extremely withdrawn or aggressive when I first encounter them in my office, but it is rare for me to not be able to complete a full evaluation. Once they've been coming for a while, it is common for them to come in easily and acquiesce to the routine of measuring their height, weight, blood pressure, and pulse and answering my sometimes inane (in their opinion) questions. I don't usually get much conversation, but I am likely to get some "yes" or "no" answers or perhaps some echolalia (immediate repetition of words spoken by another person) for the last few words of the question.

I tend to treat patients who have significant autism with multiple medications and other forms of treatment, including speech therapy, occupational therapy, and sensory therapy. It is very important to get their behavior under control so they can maintain a reasonable quality of life at home and at school.

As is typical with almost all types of autism, behavior is predictable. When families say a child's behavior changed out of nowhere, I believe the family has missed the initiating stimulus. One of the reasons the stimulus may be missed is that patients in this category may be having subtle seizures, or they may be having hallucinations, which ultimately result in an outburst.

Hallucinations can be visual or auditory. They are most easily recognized when a family member or teacher observes the patient turn toward something he thought he may have heard, but everyone else is aware that nothing is there. The atypical antipsychotic medications, which are often used in these patients for outbursts and aggression, should also be helpful for hallucinations.

Patients with moderate and severe forms of autism will often have sensory issues. These sensory issues can be a driving force for some behaviors. I had a patient with moderate to severe autism who loved the sensory stimulation of pressure. He would go the swimming pool, sink to the bottom of the deep end, and just sit there. He could stay underwater for a prolonged period of time. The new lifeguards had to be educated about this patient and his penchant for sitting on the bottom of the deep end of the pool, lest they dive in and try to "save" him.

Another common sensory issue is difficulty with loud noises, but it is not always the loudness of the noise—sometimes the pitch of the sound is intolerable. Buzzers in gymnasiums are common causes of sensory issues, especially when the patient doesn't understand when it is going to go off. Many sensory issues come with clothing, where a patient won't wear a certain item of clothing or a certain style of clothing. This issue is common and typically due to the feel of the material against the patient's skin. Even food sensitivities, often due to textures and smells, are sensory related. I had one patient who would only eat one brand of chocolate pudding. The company altered the shape of the container, and my patient would no longer eat it.

Patients with moderate autism differ from those with severe autism because they have more language and better reciprocal conversation. They still tend to have little or no social interaction, and conversation is often dominated by their favorite topic or special interest, such as dinosaurs, outer space, or orations of scenes from one of their favorite videos or TV shows. Patients will generally answer direct questions with a "yes" or a "no" or a single-word answer, but if you can find their interest, they often generate a much longer dissertation.

One unusual behavior is often seen in patients with moderate autism. If they are given a question that they do not know the answer to, they will become mute or change the subject. They rarely state, "I don't know," which seems to indicate that they feel it is not appropriate to admit that they do not know the answer to the question presented. I have a patient that is very interested in Thomas the train. When I asked him if there were any F9 diesel locomotives on Thomas the train, he answered, "Do you know steam engines use coal?" He stayed on the topic of trains and Thomas, but he did not answer my question.

Special interests can be important, especially as one considers employment. One patient, now a young adult, has a special interest in doing laundry. At 13, his father got him a front-loading washing machine for his birthday, because he knew his son would get more enjoyment out of a new washing machine than from any toy he might buy for him. For a while, this patient had a job washing the linens at a small motel near his home. This position seemed nearly ideal for him, because he could be alone in the laundry area, doing the washing with little interaction with others, accomplishing something he enjoyed that was helpful to the facility and that he could be paid for.

In this patient's case, I believe he lost his job because of company "downsizing"—it was not related to his lack of skills or personal issues. I can count on this patient always telling me, "You need a haircut." To most questions, he will respond, "I don't know." I stated previously that patients with autism spectrum disorders do not often reply with "I don't know." In this patient's case, his response doesn't always mean that he doesn't know the answer, but actually infers, "I'd rather give up than search my brain for the answer."

It is common to have difficulty finding adequate educational resources for patients with moderate and severe autism if the family does not live in or near a major metropolitan area. One of my patients resided in a small town and was in a special-education classroom with eight students and five teachers. The school complained that the child had "flipped the bird" at the teacher. They even sent a video of the episode.

In the video, which lasted about an hour, the teachers had spent less than 8 minutes in direct contact with the student. At one point, a teacher, who was working with him on handwriting, was using a hand-over-hand technique to guide his manuscript. To my amazement, while she was doing the instruction, she was talking with another teacher about a social event! My patient had no idea what "flipping the bird" meant. He was nonverbal. The most likely explanation was that he had gone to the bathroom to have a bowel movement and had not been able to get himself clean. He was reaching into his pants, finding a little fecal matter, and trying to get the teacher's attention about the fact that he needed help getting his finger and buttocks clean. The school did finally agree that he was not being aggressive.

Another patient, also from a small town, had a choice between two schools he could attend. One class was the regular classroom at his neighborhood school, which had no provisions for a special-needs student; however, the teacher had a child of her own with an autism spectrum disorder. The alternative school would require the patient to be bused to a neighboring community with a classroom for special-needs students. The teacher was a special-education teacher and had specialty training in autism.

It is typically better for a patient with an autism spectrum disorder to be in a regular classroom, if the patient is capable of learning at the regular school pace and is not too disruptive to others. When it comes to instructing a patient with an autism spectrum disorder, there is no better training for a teacher than having to deal with it on a day-to-day basis in one's own home. Therefore, in a case like this one, the local school is generally my first choice. There will need to be close monitoring by the school, the family, and me.

Another nonverbal but nonaggressive patient was entering the school system at the kindergarten level. I had hoped she could attend regular kindergarten at the neighborhood school. At the end of the very first day, the teacher approached the mother and indignantly asked, "What am I supposed to do with her?" With this teacher's attitude, it was decided that my patient should attend a special autism classroom in a neighboring community.

I have several patients with moderate or severe autism who might dart out into the street without concern for their own safety. I have had patients with moderate autism that would go into a neighbor's house, uninvited of course, and sit down and turn on the television. They watched their show, exhibiting no concern that they were not in their own home or that the neighbor might be upset with them or that their mothers would worry about where they were. The neighbors must be informed about these children, so they can also help watch out for the child's safety.

Very few patients in this category will finish high school with an academic diploma, even with a lot of support from the school and the family. They will usually live with their family or in a group home, but adequate employment as an adult is unlikely.

High-functioning autism blends into low-functioning Asperger's syndrome. I might differentiate the two on the basis of social interest and degree of impairment due to anxiety. A patient who is quite happy with no social experiences would better meet the criteria for an autism diagnosis, and the patient who wants friends, even though he isn't very good at getting or maintaining friendships, would better meet the criteria for an Asperger's syndrome diagnosis. The patient with high-functioning autism is much more likely to have fears of buzzing insects or certain noises than is a patient with low-functioning Asperger's syndrome.

The patients with high-functioning autism and low-functioning Asperger's syndrome have fairly normal speech, but pragmatics (understanding that when a person says, "Quit pulling my leg," they are aware that the other person is not actually touching them but is joking with them) and prosody (changing the tone or loudness of part of a phrase or sentence to add emphasis or alter definition) are typically not normal.

Patients in these categories may still exhibit stereotypical behaviors and special interests. Patients with high-functioning autism frequently have friends, but not typically a lot of them, and only one or two may actually call to get together or have the patient over. It is quite common that the friend will also have an autism spectrum disorder. As a matter of fact, one mother once told me that her son played so well with the neighbor kid that she was beginning to wonder about the neighbor kid and whether he might have an autism spectrum disorder, as well!

Families who live with a family member who has autism are typically very insightful when it comes to autistic spectrum behavioral symptoms in others. I had a patient who had been referred to me for an evaluation by a teacher who had a child with an autism spectrum disorder. The teacher suspected an autism spectrum disorder in this student. At the initial evaluation, I wasn't really sure that an autism spectrum disorder was the correct diagnosis. I asked the child's mother to contact his teacher and ask him to send me a note about what the teacher had seen that concerned him about autism. The teacher's observations, along with repeated evaluations of the child and my own observations about his response to medication, eventually defined the diagnosis of an autism spectrum disorder. It was a mild disorder and could easily have been missed without the interest of his teacher.

The best education on the autism spectrum and the behaviors involved is obtained by living with a person with an autistic spectrum disorder, even though they are not all alike. A patient who is in college asked me, "If I had a best friend in elementary school who had autism, would that make me more likely to have autistic features?" I answered that I didn't believe so, but his ability to maintain a friendship with a child with autism may have been easier if he had some autistic features of his own.

Perhaps the best teacher for a child with an autistic spectrum disorder is a teacher who has a child on the spectrum. Most teachers can teach a student on the spectrum without having to live with someone on the spectrum, but a teacher who has had personal experience with his or her own child with autism may be better able to understand the limits of motivating the student and encouraging progress without unduly provoking anxiety. Teachers and parents almost always have to push and encourage a student with an autism spectrum disorder, or the patient is likely to maintain only the status quo. The ability to encourage work without markedly provoking stress is one of the keys to academic success in many patients with an autism spectrum disorder.

Patients in these categories, both high-functioning autism and low-functioning Asperger's syndrome, do hold jobs. They are often quite capable of doing the work. They are reliable about showing up for work and often arrive early. Difficulties with continued employment most often relate to difficulties with management or coworker relationships, rather than an inability to do the job.

However, training for many jobs is not completely explained, and then the patient may unknowingly get into trouble. For example, one of my patients had a job working in a small business that packaged materials for shipping for other small businesses. My patient was fired because his employer thought he was lazy, but I suspect that my patient was never told what other chores to do if there was nothing in front of him to package.

Patients may have difficulty staying on task when conversing with a coworker. I had a patient who had gotten a landscaping job at a factory, where a relative of his was employed. His probationary period had to be extended beyond the initial 90 days, because he was talking to coworkers for too long during work hours. My patient's adjustment, which he figured out on his own, was to only talk with his coworkers during his breaks, because his skills were poor at gauging how long he had been talking or knowing how to look busy while engaged in a conversation.

Patients with this level of autism and Asperger's syndrome do drive automobiles, although they typically just drive to work or school and then home again. I have a patient who bought a new car 2½ years ago. He recently told me he's only put 9,000 miles on the car. It is also common to see these patients go to work and come home only to eat, sleep, watch TV, and play video games. There tends to be little planning for the future, and they tend to live very much in the moment, focused on their own immediate entertainment.

Patients at this level do engage in sexual relationships. I had a patient, a 25-year-old girl, who was having sex with a boy who also had autism. This was accomplished mostly with parental knowledge and sometimes not. I asked her if she took birth control pills, and she said, "Yes." I inquired, "Well, does he use anything?" "Yes, he uses a condom." Not willing to let it go at that, I asked, "Does he put it on, or do you put it on him?" "He puts it on." I further questioned, "So he comes in, takes off his clothes, and puts on the condom?" "Oh, we don't take off our clothes!" she said. As it turns out, they did take off enough clothing to have sex, but they did not realize that most people get naked first.

This conversation presents a lesson to all of us. A lot of behaviors that seem obvious and innate to most persons are not necessarily obvious to patients with autism spectrum disorders. It is my job and that of the families to help the patient with the unwritten rules and behaviors of the world of typical development. It is difficult for many who are not acquainted with autistic behaviors to understand how such a simple concept could be misunderstood.

Patients in this category may attend college, but they are more likely to enroll in a local community college than a large university. Some patients can do quite well academically in some courses of study, if it is an area of high interest or if understanding of the subject matter comes easily to them. But, patients in this category have great trouble with time management and dividing up study time between subjects. They tend to be more willing to spend time on the subject they know the best, rather than the one they know the least.

It seems to be difficult for a patient with high-functioning autism to understand why one would write a paper or study for a test several days in advance of its due date. Seeking outside help may be much more necessary to improve organization and time management than getting direct academic help, although both will likely be called for.

I have had another small group of patients who were able to make honor roll grades in difficult courses at difficult colleges, without having to study. They did go to class and they did do the homework, but they were smart enough that they did not have to go back and review the material for a test. One of my patients graduated with all "A's" and "B's" at a difficult college, without studying. His major was chemistry. He attended class and did the homework, but he preferred reading nonacademic literature to studying.

I had a patient who was a "straight-A" student at a difficult parochial, college-prep high school. When she went to get her driver's license, she earned an "A" in the written work, but she failed her in car driving test four times. When she was brought in for an evaluation with a specialist on driving, it was found that she was trying to watch too many things. She had to be taught what to watch and how to prioritize what she was seeing. Once she learned those skills, she was successful at learning to drive, and now she drives without difficulty.

Patients with autism spectrum disorders frequently have decreased proprioception and sometimes have underdeveloped fine-motor control. Proprioception refers to the ability to sense what a part of one's body is doing without having to see it. For example, I can raise my arm above my head and tap my fingers together on that hand, and I know which fingers I am tapping together without having to look at my hand. Patients with an autism spectrum disorder often, but not always, have decreased proprioception. Proprioception may improve with age without any intervention, but occupational and physical therapy may be considered. When a person has poor proprioception, he is often seen as being

somewhat clumsy. Patients with poor proprioception don't always know how far down a stair step
is or how close they are to a wall or a piece of fur-
niture. Many years ago, I had a patient who would
turn sideways when he went through a doorway,
because he had a poor sense of how close his
shoulders were to the doorframe.

Poor proprioception may be a consideration
when it comes to picking a musical instrument
to play. Playing a trumpet or a saxophone, where
your fingers stay mostly stationary, would be
less dependent on having good proprioception
than playing a guitar or a violin, where your
finger positioning is critical. Playing percussion
doesn't typically require a lot of proprioceptive
ability or fine-motor control until one begins to
play the marimba or xylophone, and, therefore,
may be a good choice for a patient with proprioceptive issues.

Many of my patients will not attend a live
sporting event or even watch one on television.
Most patients in this category do not play team
sports, although there are a few who do, and
they may excel. For example, Moe Norman was a
professional PGA golfer who almost certainly had
an autism spectrum disorder. His swing lasted
the same portion of a second every time he hit

a shot. He could easily hit the ball straight and didn't understand why others did not. Being able to have an exactly repeatable swing would be a major advantage in a sport such as golf.

As another example, I had a patient who was a statewide champion in karate. To him, it was easy to visually remember the exact arm and leg positions he was to present. Having a strong visual memory is not uncommon in autism spectrum disorders. Dr Temple Grandin has written a book on visual memory in autism entitled, *Thinking in Pictures.*

Typically, the student with an autism spectrum disorder lacks skills and interest in sports. Many of my patients will not watch sports, but a few are sports fanatics. I have many patients who are fans of NASCAR racing. Their incidental memory is so good that they can tell the cars apart from each racing season, just by looking at a picture or a model of the car.

In many sports, however, they may not understand the concept of winning as a team and what their role might be in accomplishing a win for their team. They can create problems with their teammates when they correct a teammate, even though they themselves often make a similar error. I had a patient that was in Little League baseball, who told a teammate that he wouldn't get thrown out at first base as often if he lost weight. His statement was true enough, but my patient did not feel he was fairly treated when he received a two-game suspension for trying to be helpful.

Patients with autism spectrum disorders rarely tolerate a coach or teacher being "in their face." They often recoil in fear when a teacher or coach has reprimanded them. It would not be rare for patients to complain that a teacher, coach, or parent was yelling at them, when indeed the adult was just being corrective and was neither being loud nor raising his or her voice.

Patients with autism spectrum disorders often require some nudging or prodding to improve performance or take on new challenges. If there is a teacher or a coach who is reluctant to push the patient, fearing it may result in an increase in anxiety, the student will have the upper hand and do little. I frequently remind families, "If you think he isn't smart enough to manipulate the situation, you're in big trouble."

Having difficulty with correction, especially if it is aggressive or "in your face," is also a major problem with regard to military training. I have had some patients with Asperger's syndrome

and a higher level of functioning who stop taking
their medications and go into military service.
Some do well, but many do not and are susceptible to mental breakdowns with the rigors of
military basic training. If they can be successful,
they often find security in the black-and-white
nature of the military and the carefully explained
directions for a particular job or area. Constant,
strict routine is typically reassuring for patients
with an autism spectrum disorder. Looking at it
from the other way around, they have a lack of
tolerance for uncertainty, which I believe is anxiety driven.

Patients with severe, moderate, and high-functioning autism experience enough difficulties that
they typically do consult with a professional for
help. The diagnosis is often fairly straightforward,
and multiple treatment strategies will be required.

Asperger's Syndrome

In 1944, Hans Asperger published an article in Vienna that described the characteristics of four boys he had been treating. Hans Asperger and Leo Kanner, whose article on autism was published in 1943, were apparently not aware of each other's work. Dr Asperger's article was published in Austria at the time of the war. Its presence was little known to the western world until Dr Lorna Wing began to look at it in England in the early 1980s. Some of the characteristics are similar to high-functioning autism, but two major distinctions were described. Dr Asperger stated that, in his patients, there was no major language delay and no significant cognitive delay. Strictly speaking, if a patient has any language delay, the patient does not meet the criteria for Asperger's syndrome and should receive a diagnosis of PDD-NOS.

As I stated previously, I often see patients who have a history of a 1- to 3-year language delay, who, by the age of 8 or 9 years, have pretty good reciprocal conversation and seem to be identical to children with a diagnosis of Asperger's syndrome. I am more likely to diagnose these cases as Asperger's syndrome than PDD-NOS.

Although many families would rather receive a diagnosis of Asperger's syndrome than autism, most families are interested in what can be done to improve the patient's symptoms and want to know if there is a possibility of predicting what the patient's situation might look like as a young adult.

"Is he going to get married?" "Is he going to go to college and move out?" These are common and serious questions families ask as they try to plan for the future. I often tell families that they will want the patient to marry someone with no autism in their family history, owing to genetic concerns. What the family hears is that I think the patient is going to get married.

I divide Asperger's syndrome into five categories: high functioning, moderately high functioning, moderate functioning, moderately low functioning, and low functioning. These are not official categories, and I sort the patient's diagnosis on the basis of difficulties with school, familial interaction, social issues, anxiety, and language. Patients with mild impairment would likely only have issues in one, or, at the most, two of these areas. For example, there may be mild issues with grades at school and mild social issues with peers. Patients who are more severely impaired will have difficulties in all five areas of functioning.

High-Functioning Asperger's Syndrome

Patients with high-functioning Asperger's syndrome rarely come in to see me for diagnosis or treatment. For the most part, they are able to function well without any outside help. A diagnosis is considered when I am treating a more significantly affected sibling, and the patient's mother begins to recognize mild symptoms in the previously undiagnosed sibling.

I have a patient who fits this category and is now a young woman. When she was in middle school, I believed she had Asperger's syndrome, but I could not convince anyone else, including an excellent psychologist who is very adept at counseling and testing patients with autism spectrum disorders.

One day, the patient was sitting in my office with her mother. She has always been a very attractive young lady. That day, she was wearing her cheerleader outfit. At the time, she was a sophomore in high school. In a further attempt to define her issues, I asked her, in front of her mother, "How are you at flirting?" She gave me the answer that I feel is most typical of patients with Asperger's syndrome, which is, "I don't know." She's not saying she doesn't know how to flirt—she's seen others do it—but she isn't certain how to assess its effects.

A girl's mother doesn't typically sit her down and teach her child how to flirt; most girls innately know how to do it and how to assess its effects. In autism spectrum disorders, patients may have to be helped or taught both how to flirt and how to assess its effects. Many males with Asperger's syndrome are oblivious that a girl has an interest in them, because they don't pick up on the nonverbal cues. These same males may also assume that a girl is very interested in them as a boyfriend, when the girl is simply being social or nice to them and has no relationship interest. I also see patients who, once they do have a girlfriend, tend to be too smothering, wanting to have or give almost constant attention. This smothering often results in a discontinuation of the relationship.

As bad as men are at knowing what women want men to do, males with Asperger's syndrome are worse. I tell their spouses, "Don't tell your husband he needs to spend more time with the kids—tell him he's taking the kids to a particular movie at 2 o'clock on Saturday. He'll do it!" This is even good advice for mothers who don't have a child or a husband with an autism spectrum disorder.

Here is another story of a female patient with high-functioning Asperger's syndrome. In middle school, she came to her mother and complained that she didn't have many friends. Her mother told her, "Your sister has friends—do what she does." She studied her sister for 2½ weeks and became "Miss Social." It was a façade. It didn't hold up in college when her boyfriend dumped her during finals week. Her sister was aware that the girl's boyfriend was using her, but the patient didn't know he was.

She subsequently became depressed and started taking an antidepressant. Her mother related that, after starting to take medications, she had begun clearing her plate from the table when she got up from a meal. Even prior to taking medications, if she had been asked to clear the table, she would have done it and done a good job. However, prior to starting medication, it had never occurred to her that clearing her dishes from the table when she got up would be helpful to her mother.

Patients with high-functioning Asperger's syndrome are not without friends, and all of their symptoms tend to be mild. Most patients in this category do not require treatment with medication, but one should always watch for issues concerning anxiety.

In many of my patients' parents, a diagnosis of high-functioning or moderately high-functioning Asperger's syndrome would apply. When I diagnose Asperger's syndrome, there is some discussion about other family members who might also be affected. It would not be rare for one of the implicated family members to be the father of the patient. Eventually, the mother realizes that a mild autism spectrum disorder exists in her partner and may be the reason why he doesn't pick up on her needs or why he corrects her constantly or buys her overly practical gifts that always seem to have electric cords— and that he isn't likely to change. However, an interesting observation is that I have rarely seen that information lead to the end of the marriage. There must be an affection and tolerance that holds the marriage together, in spite of a partner's social issues. High-functioning Asperger's syndrome is not limited to just females; males can also populate this category.

Moderately High-Functioning Asperger's Syndrome

Patients with moderately high-functioning Asperger's syndrome have just a bit more difficulty than patients with high-functioning Asperger's syndrome and perhaps in more than one area. Mild symptoms might be impairment in school, work, or social relationships. Typically, there are not a lot of anxiety issues.

Most patients with Asperger's syndrome, particularly at the upper levels, are capable of achieving success in college, but they are not always interested in leaving home to attend college. They may not even be interested in attending a college in the local community, while living at home. Most patients with the upper levels of Asperger's syndrome manage dating and sexual relationships. For example, I have a patient who is a junior in college. He has had a steady girlfriend for about 6 months, they are sexually active, and the relationship is going well. Prior to this relationship, he had only dated one other girl. That relationship lasted for 2 years in high school. Because he really wasn't certain why that relationship had broken up, he would not be able to prevent himself from having similar problems in his current relationship.

His academic problems were limited to maintaining attention and prioritizing time. He had made several friends at college and seemed to be enjoying college life. He did have some disdain for other students who would drink themselves into a stupor, but I have seen this disdain in patients without an autism spectrum disorder. He would drink alcohol, but not typically to the excess that might be seen in many males of college age. Being somewhat rigid about rules and naive about overlooking certain social behaviors and bending the rules is common in patients with autism spectrum disorders.

Several years ago, I evaluated a new patient who was 17 years of age and a junior in high school. He had gotten through school fairly well, but he didn't have very many friends. He wanted nothing to do with my diagnosis of Asperger's syndrome or my treatment. I said to him, "You know, if people don't want to be your friend, they won't tell you why." He replied, "Why not, that would help me!" This statement might be typical of patients with moderate to moderately high-functioning Asperger's syndrome. They are aware that they are having social difficulty and would like to have a "guardian angel" on their shoulder to inform them of why a particular encounter did not go well and how the situation might be improved the next time.

Some desperation may be seen when a relationship is breaking up with a partner who has been helpful as a "guardian angel" and is now ending the relationship. The patient is quite aware that the partner has, and would, help him in the future with understanding social interaction and conversation, if the relationship were to continue.

A patient who doesn't seek treatment until his late teens will likely be a patient who has a higher level of Asperger's syndrome or PDD-NOS, if he does meet the criteria for an autism spectrum disorder. Patients with more significant issues should receive diagnoses at an earlier age. The exception is when the patient has received a diagnosis of a similar condition, such as Tourette syndrome or bipolar disorder, and the autistic spectrum disorder has been overlooked. I have evaluated two patients, previously with diagnoses of Tourette syndrome, whom I thought had Asperger's syndrome. Typically, Asperger's syndrome and Tourette syndrome would not be confused, because patients with autism spectrum disorders do not commonly have tics—but both diagnoses share a high incidence of issues with ADHD and anxiety.

I remember evaluating a young teenaged boy who was having a lot of tics, but he was clearly a patient on the autistic spectrum. His father was in the room during the physical exam and did not exhibit tics. After the physical exam, the mother was brought into the room, and it was obvious from whom the tics had come. The tics were something else he had inherited, along with his autism. It is not rare for patients with autism spectrum disorders to have tics, but it is also not common. Tics can be aggravated and improved with medications.

Patients with this level of functioning will probably finish college and should be able to obtain employment in their chosen field; however, there may be problems with interviewing when they are trying to obtain employment in the first place. I have a patient who, when asked during an interview what salary he was looking for, answered, "At least twelve dollars an hour." He had recently finished college and should have been asking for $30,000 to $50,000 dollars a year!

I also had a patient who made good grades in hotel management at a prominent university. I had suggested that hotel management might not be a good field for her, with her Asperger's syndrome, but she tried to reassure me that she was learning how to work around her difficulties. As it turns out, she has never been able to get a job in her chosen field, and I do not know what has prevented her from achieving appropriate employment in the hotel industry. I suspect she has difficulties with interview skills and maintaining good eye contact.

She has been able to obtain employment in the mortgage industry, but she has seldom stayed in one job for much over 1½ years. She has lost her employment for various reasons. Once, she was dating a man who was a member of the family who owned the business she worked for. When he grew tired of their relationship, he fired her. She had believed that he would protect her job, and she had not recognized that her employment might be in jeopardy if he tired of her. Complaints centered on the pace of her work and her somewhat relentless questioning about being shown how she was supposed to do projects to her employer's satisfaction. As I mentioned previously, many duties are not explained completely, and the employee is supposed to figure out how to accomplish the end result on his or her own. This particular patient seemed to exhibit moderate difficulty with meeting her employer's demands without having to ask for what the employer believed to be too much reassurance and instruction.

Many patients in this category will marry and have children. The patient just described became pregnant and seemed to do a good job of caring for her son as a single parent, but she did have good familial support from her parents and siblings. She continued taking her medications for ADHD and anxiety.

For adults with an autism spectrum disorder, two problems are common as a marriage partner and parent. As I stated previously, most men are not very good at understanding what women want them to do. This is especially so in men with Asperger's syndrome. They may also not understand why a certain statement was offensive to their partner. A statement offered up as just a statement of fact in his mind may carry an offensive connotation that was neither foreseen nor intended.

An example similar to this occurred in my own life. I was sanding drywall above a large mirror in a bathroom. The large mirror was difficult to remove, and so, instead of removing it, I just put masking tape across the top of the mirror to keep any dust from getting behind it. A friend saw what I was doing and asked why I had not removed the mirror. I pointed out that I had put up the masking tape to keep the dust from falling behind the mirror, and she stated, "A woman wouldn't have done it that way." To her, she was simply stating a fact; to me, she was being demeaning.

In adults who are parents and have autism spectrum disorders, I see difficulties with a lack of flexibility concerning child behavior and discipline. I commonly see or hear about Dad (in this case the parent who has some degree of Asperger's syndrome) trying to strictly enforce a rule with a child. He becomes upset when his spouse takes a softer or even protective stance toward the child, as she believes there may have been extenuating circumstances that led to the behavior in question. Dad may become very upset, because that is not the way it was done when he was growing up. When he was young, one had to do exactly as he was told, or there would be a punishment. It will often be up to the talents of the mother to step in between the father and the child to balance the "black and white" interpretations of her spouse and the behavioral issues of her child. Having to get between her husband and the child may exacerbate marriage difficulties and is a chore that few mothers enjoy.

Moderate Asperger's Syndrome

Patients with moderate Asperger's syndrome typically have difficulties in more than one aspect of their lives, including academics, social interactions, family interactions, and overall anxiety. Academics are often affected, but for a few different reasons. The patient may not be working on a subject because he just doesn't see the importance of that class to his life or his academic career. We all find it easier to work hard on a subject that we enjoy, but the difference is we can still manage a reasonable effort, even if we don't. Patients with Asperger's syndrome may have such an aversion to a particular subject that they are unable to do the work, although they may attend class.

I had a patient in college whose major was chemistry, and he found it very difficult to do schoolwork because, scientifically speaking, learning may just be about "electrons moving around in his brain." Another student, also in college, had convinced himself that the "end time" was coming soon; therefore, there was no need to attend school. He quit school in the middle of the term, except for choir. When I asked him what he was doing with his time, expecting that he may be studying the Bible or praying, he replied that he was hanging out with friends and playing video games. Of course, he didn't feel the need to find a job with the demise of the world so close.

Another issue might be that the student doesn't like the teacher. I see many patients with upper levels of Asperger's syndrome who are not performing well in school, because the teacher has given up on them. The teacher believes the student is not being successful on purpose or is being lazy and manipulative. The teacher may also believe that the child's mother and I are just being buffaloed by the child.

Often, the teacher has seen that the student is capable of doing better work and is trying to get him to do it. The student doesn't realize the teacher is trying to get him to work harder; he believes she dislikes him, and, therefore, he dislikes her. I have a family that was attending an Individualized Educational Program (IEP) meeting at school, and a teacher blurted out that the student was just a big manipulator and didn't deserve an IEP. My patient has moderately high-functioning Asperger's syndrome, and an IEP is clearly appropriate.

The patient may not be doing his work because he believes the teacher dislikes him and has it out for him. I had a patient who was a teenager in high school and complained about a teacher that, if the patient asked for assistance, would merely suggest that he work harder to look up whatever he needed. Another student in his class, who was much less capable and also a patient of mine, would ask for and receive more direct assistance from the teacher. This "unfairness" aggravated the first patient greatly, and he would do little for that teacher. It ended up being such a pervasive problem that the family changed schools.

There may also be educational difficulties related to problems with abstraction of information, which is due to the language-based learning disability that is part of an autism spectrum disorder. This is particularly evident at the middle school and high school levels. If a test question asks for the date George Washington crossed the Delaware, most patients know the answer, if the information was in the study guide. If the question asks the student to explain *why* Washington crossed the Delaware, based on the information given in the chapter, they often have more difficulty and easily give up or respond with very brief answers.

Difficulty with abstraction of information in patients with Asperger's syndrome and autism is related to the language-based learning disability, which I believe is inherent to the disorder. Patients have to work harder to figure out how to work around their problems. Spelling and decoding words can be easy, but figuring out the most salient information or how to abstract information to answer the teacher's question correctly may be extraordinarily difficult.

This language-based learning difficulty also makes it difficult for the patient to evaluate why the teacher was not pleased with the answer given. To the student, the terse answer included all the information required. I have seen this be an issue even at the college level with some patients, although, if they are in college, they have usually figured out how to work around this problem.

Many patients who have difficulty with various aspects of learning must put forth extra effort to overcome their challenges. However, most of my patients are not interested in putting forth extra effort. Teachers often complain that the student does not ask for help when he is having trouble. The student does not ask for clarification of information or directions because he believes he's "gotten it." If another student asks for clarification of a concept and the clarification is given, then my patient will realize he did not understand the concept correctly. He never would have asked for clarification on his own, because he was unaware he did not learn or understand the concept properly.

On occasion, patients like this might also do well with little or no studying, but then they can perform poorly even after a lengthy but ineffective study period. If they do not make the connection between ineffective studying and poor test results, they will not see the need for focused studying.

The patient may be having difficulty with attention because he isn't taking the best medicine or the best dosage for his ADHD, or he is refusing to take it. Some ADHD medications are more helpful for getting things in or out of memory than other medications. Some medications can make a patient so focused that he cannot let go of a certain question or concept, and he subsequently runs out of time. In art class, the ADHD medication may make the patient so focused on perfection that he cannot finish his piece of art on time and turn it in for credit. I had a patient with moderately high-functioning Asperger's syndrome who drew incredible political cartoons for the high-school newspaper, but he was flunking out of a prestigious school of art because he only wanted to create the art he wanted to do. Even on a piece of artwork that he was willing to do, he would have difficulty stopping and turning it in for credit.

Patients in this category are targets for bullies, especially at the middle-school level. Bullying does seem to lessen by high school and is markedly less common at the college level. But, even the workplace can be a setup for these patients and adult bullies. Others may not know what the diagnosis is, but they do know they can set up the patient to get upset or get in trouble with management or a coworker. Even though bullying is uncomfortable for the patients, I do not believe they should be removed from school to protect them from it. Instead, they should be helped by the school and the family to get through it. One of my patients who had moderate Asperger's syndrome and attended a somewhat rough school made friends with a great big football player, and he was no longer bullied.

Moderately Low-Functioning Asperger's Syndrome

Patients with moderately low-functioning Asperger's syndrome are going to have significant social, academic, and anxiety issues. They will do better than patients with high-functioning autism, and they might develop a few friends on the basis of similar interests. At this level of Asperger's syndrome, friends make friends on the basis of similar interests. In this day and age, it is almost always the playing of video games that is the shared interest. The problem is the child may want his friend to come over and mostly sit there and watch him play a video game. Sometimes this does work, especially if the friend is also on the autistic spectrum, but even kids with autism spectrum disorders want to participate in the play activity. Normally developing children will rarely accept this type of social interaction and end up going home or playing with the host's sibling.

I have seen female patients with moderately low-functioning Asperger's syndrome who could not have a steady boyfriend because they could not tolerate someone else touching them, especially in a sexual manner. This type of sensory sensitivity may show up at an appointment, when the patient cringes away as I start to place the blood pressure cuff on her arm. I believe anxiety drives this somewhat typical aversion to touch in patients with autism spectrum disorders.

Sometimes the skin can be so sensitive that the patients consider touch painful. It is not possible to lower the sensitivity of the skin or the other senses with medications. I can decrease the anxiety about the upcoming event that is likely to occur or help her learn to let touch "roll off her back" more easily. Many females will tell me that it will all be okay once they find just the right partner. However, most females I have treated with this level of Asperger's syndrome never seem to find the right partner.

Low-Functioning Asperger's Syndrome

Low-functioning Asperger's syndrome is similar to high-functioning autism, except that language usage and reciprocal conversation are better in patients with Asperger's syndrome. There are likely to be significant academic issues, and a lot of those academic issues will be related to the patient focusing only on what the patient wants to do, rather than on what he needs to do.

Patients with high-functioning autism may not have friends, but they seem to not care. Patients with low-functioning Asperger's syndrome may not have friends, but they are much more likely to be upset about their lack of friends and their inability to attract and keep friends. I typically advise parents to try and get the patient into a group of kids who have similar skills or interests, such as scouting or karate, to attempt to make friends.

I have one patient who is very interested in gaming. I can be sure that whenever the Gen Com game convention is held in Indianapolis, she is going to make an appointment to see me. Her entire family comes for the convention. It might be a good place for her to make friends with similar interests, but she seems to stay pretty close to her family members, rather than befriending some of the other convention attendees.

Another patient in my practice, who most likely has high-functioning autism (although some would believe he has Asperger's syndrome), is now 19 years old. His family and I were discussing the probability of him driving an automobile. His parents were concerned that he might be easily distracted by the thoughts going through his head and lose track of the fact that he is the one who is driving the car. Obviously, that could have disastrous results.

A professional must heed a family's insights into behavior when looking at school, driving, employment, and, really, all aspects of social interaction when guiding treatments and giving advice. After all, the patient's family sees him every day, and they know him the best. My patients with autism spectrum disorders are usually cautious drivers compared with my patients with ADHD, who tend to be aggressive drivers. My patients still have problems with driving, getting tickets, and getting into accidents, but not typically because of excessive speed.

Not too long ago, however, I had a patient with Asperger's syndrome who did get stopped for speeding. The officer asked my patient if he knew how fast he was going, and he answered, "Yes." The officer then asked if my patient was trying to be smart with him, and he answered, "Yes." These answers are examples of pragmatic errors commonly seen in patients with autism spectrum disorders. Fortunately, my patient did not get in trouble with the officer for what might be considered smart-aleck remarks. The patient believed he was responding with good, appropriate answers.

There are some computerized driving simulators that provide a good evaluation of a patient's ability to maintain focus and be aware of signage and other vehicles during a driving simulation. The results are quite complete and impressive, but the testing is slightly expensive. However, this testing can be very helpful in reassuring both the family and the patient that driving is indeed a reasonable goal.

Global positioning units or in-car satellite navigation systems can be invaluable if the patient encounters a detour or gets lost. I have a patient who went out to a restaurant close to home for a hamburger and fries. He took the wrong ramp and ended up in a town 40 miles away before he realized his mistake. He did not have a navigation system, and his parents had to keep him on the phone while he was driving to guide him back home.

Here's another example of a pragmatic error. A fifth-grade patient was asked to write down how he solved a math story problem. His answer was, "I thought very hard with my brain." A few questions later, he replied with the same answer, "I thought very hard with my brain, as I did in question number three." The teacher gave him credit for his answers, even though she had wanted for him to show the written work he did to solve the math problem.

Chapter

6

Medications

Medications

are used to treat symptoms associated with autism spectrum disorders. It is easier to understand why a certain medication might be used if one understands what drives the problematic behavior or symptom. I define an autism spectrum disorder as a syndrome that includes a combination of ADHD, anxiety, and a language-based learning disability. The language-based learning disability causes patients to take language too literally and not read body language well, if at all. Even if they do read nonverbal language correctly, it may not alter their behavior.

There have been several articles published over the past few years that discuss the co-morbid or co-occurring psychiatric diagnoses in patients with autism spectrum disorders. The most commonly brought up co-morbidities are ADHD, obsessive-compulsive disorder, anxiety disorders, oppositional defiant disorder, and depression. With my experience, I believe that ADHD and anxiety disorders are not co-morbid conditions seen with Asperger's syndrome and autism, but rather are integral parts of the disorders. I also believe that anxiety is a major driver of many problematic behaviors in patients with autism and Asperger's syndrome.

It has also been my frequent observation that families do not have an understanding of anxiety as a driver of behavior. Families do recognize panic, but they do not recognize that a patient's need for sameness is anxiety driven. The need to correct the parent or teacher is anxiety driven. Trouble with maintaining attention in class may be anxiety driven. The child may be worried about how the rest of the day will go. Is Mom okay? What video game am I going to play when I get home? Is Daddy going to be angry with me? Is the bully going to be on the bus today?

Anxiety may also be the cause of long pauses in communication, when the patient is trying to find the exact word to express what he is trying to say or is trying to find exactly the answer he thinks the listener wants. High anxiety is a common cause of poor sleep initiation and maintenance. Lying there pondering your troubles is not a good way to relax and fall asleep. Since poor sleep quality and quantity aggravate both ADHD and anxiety, a vicious cycle is created, with less sleep, more anxiety, less sleep, and so on.

Patients with autism spectrum disorders have poor tolerance for uncertainty, and this intolerance is anxiety driven. It is the lack of tolerance for uncertainty that makes new situations frightening or new foods difficult to try. Anxiety is what causes concern in a preschooler when Mom does not take the usual route to preschool. Most patients with autism spectrum disorders remember almost everything they experience (incidental memories), and, therefore, they know that Mom is not following the usual route, even at a very young age. A 2-year-old may tell Mom that she is not taking the correct road to Grandma's house or preschool.

Anxiety can be treated with medications, and it can be treated with cognitive behavioral therapy. In typically developing patients with anxiety, both treatments have been shown to be effective, but cognitive behavioral therapy may be effective for longer periods of time. At this time, it is common practice to use both medication and cognitive behavioral therapy together, especially at the beginning of treatment. I have not found that cognitive behavioral therapy is as effective in patients with autistic spectrum disorders as in typically developing patients. I believe this lack of response is primarily due to the fact that the patients with autism spectrum disorders have trouble transferring the lessons learned from one paradigm to another. If the new paradigm isn't almost identical to the paradigm learned, the patient may not see the relevance and may fail to invoke the lesson learned.

There are studies that support the use of cognitive behavioral therapy in autism spectrum disorders, but I suspect it is most effective in the milder cases and requires a therapist who is extremely familiar with autistic thinking. I am not saying that cognitive behavioral therapy shouldn't be used with autism spectrum disorders; I'm only saying that the results are usually less impressive than they are in typically developing patients. Cognitive behavioral therapy is likely to be most effective in the patients on the spectrum who are the highest functioning.

The medications I use the most for anxiety are the selective serotonin reuptake inhibitors (SSRIs). They are typically very effective and have a minimum of side effects. Fluoxetine (trade name Prozac) and sertraline (trade name Zoloft) have been approved by the FDA for use in children, adolescents, and adults and are therefore preferred. Escitalopram (trade name Lexapro) has been approved in adults and adolescents down to the age of 12.

Paroxetine (trade name Paxil) is not approved for use in children at this time, but there are medical studies that support its effectiveness and usage in youth. Paroxetine may have a very short half-life in children, and I rarely prescribe it. The half-life of a medication relates to how long it takes for one's body to process one half of the dose. A medicine like aspirin has a very short half-life and is therefore only effective for a few hours. Fluoxetine has a half-life of a few days in adults and will last long enough that it could be dosed only once or twice a week.

Children generally metabolize medications much more quickly than do adults, and this is a major consideration when establishing an adequate and effective dosage in children. Somewhere near puberty or thereafter, children begin to metabolize medications as adults do, but, even in adults, there is a range of metabolic turnover, so not all 160-lb patients will take the same dose of a certain medication. Final dosing of these medications is often more related to how fast the patient metabolizes it, rather than how bad their symptoms are or how much they weigh.

It is not that one SSRI is a lot stronger than another, within the group now available, but some patients may definitely get better results with one medication than with another, and that outcome is not related to the strength of the medication. The cause of a better effect is not understood at this time. In simple terms, SSRIs do not add serotonin to the brain, but they inhibit recycling of serotonin by a neuron, so the end result is stronger chemical transmission from one neuron to another.

Side effects with SSRI medications are usually mild. There may be effects on appetite, both increased and decreased, but they are usually minimal, except with mirtazapine (trade name Remeron) and paroxetine (trade name Paxil), which are likely to increase appetite. Mirtazapine also is likely to make patients sleepy, and, therefore, it is most often taken in the evening. Both of these side effects make it a useful agent when a patient experiences difficulty with falling asleep, along with poor appetite, which may be seen when a patient is also being treated for ADHD with a stimulant medication. It is also made in an orally dissolvable tablet (a tablet that is meant to dissolve in the mouth rather than to be swallowed), which makes it useful when a patient cannot or will not swallow. I treated a young patient who could swallow medications, but he would almost always vomit them back up. Mirtazapine (trade name Remeron) was very helpful for this patient, because it is absorbed through the membranes of the mouth, and there is nothing to vomit up. It increased his appetite, and, with the lowering of anxiety, he was able to eat a wider variety of foods.

Dry mouth is a side effect of almost every medication that I use. Children and adolescents rarely complain about dry mouth, but it is a frequent complaint in adults. I did have a unique situation when a patient I was treating had trouble keeping her oboe reeds moist, secondary to the drying effects of her medication. Most patients will ease their dry mouth by sipping liquids frequently, but, in some patients, excessive dry mouth may be a reason to consider a medication change.

Sexual side effects, typically decreased libido or difficulties reaching orgasm, seem to occur rarely in children and adolescents. Some parents would like for their teen to have a decreased sexual appetite, but I rarely see it. I have seen sexual difficulties in young adults, however, and it is quite common in older adults. This side effect is rarely tolerated by patients for a lengthy period of time.

I had a patient, a college coed, who took a combination of four medications for her Asperger's syndrome. One summer, while vacationing out of state with her boyfriend, she acutely quit taking all her medications. Fortunately, she did not become ill. There may be significant problems with rapid withdrawal of some of these medications, particularly if the dose is high.

After summer vacation she decided to restart her medications, although she couldn't tell me why she made that decision. When she restarted them, however, she began taking her previous full dose, and that is when she became ill. This particular patient attended a small college, with only 400 on-campus students, and when she became sick, she did not go to class for 3 weeks. During that time, no one checked on her. The school had been informed about her Asperger's syndrome, and she had signed a release that the school could confer directly with her parents. No one called her family (but, this cannot be said of all schools). Evidently, her original impetus for stopping her medications was the sexual side effects. After I was made aware of her issues, I was able to alter her medications to minimize those side effects.

Another college student at a different university was doing poorly in school, and his school called his father during spring break to inform him that they did not think his son was performing at a level that would allow him to continue as a student at that school. They did not believe it was an academic issue, but they were concerned that he was depressed. Two days later, I saw this patient, and he had moderate depression and was considering suicide. This school had started a program to teach professors the signs and symptoms of psychiatric issues, hopefully at an early stage, and then to inform someone within the program about their concerns, which ultimately benefits the student. The program was definitely beneficial to my patient, although he did have to drop out of school for a while.

Goals of SSRI medication treatment in autism and Asperger's syndrome are threefold. The first level of effect is to decrease anxiety and obsessive-compulsive behavior and to ease transitions. This should happen—that's what these medications are for. But, dosages may have to be much higher for obsessive-compulsive behavior than for mild anxiety. As discussed previously, anxiety is a driving force for many behaviors and issues seen in a child, adolescent, or adult with an autism spectrum disorder. Meltdowns are typically driven by anxiety. I see patients who have several meltdowns a day, and, with adequate treatment with an SSRI, meltdowns might be reduced to once or twice a month. When the patient does have a meltdown, it becomes easier for the patient or family to shorten it or decrease its severity.

Obsessive behaviors and even stereotypies may be aggravated by anxiety. One may see a significant decrease in their occurrence with an SSRI; however, some obsessive behaviors are simply habits, and stereotypies can also be seen in times of boredom and excitement. It is not always clear how much reduction of a behavior might be achieved. There may be a situation where the SSRI has decreased the incidence of meltdowns, but it becomes necessary to address another concern, such as ADHD. The dose of the SSRI can be maintained, the ADHD is addressed, often with a stimulant medication that may aggravate anxiety, and, subsequently, the SSRI dosage will have to be adjusted to achieve maximum benefit for the patient. This will be discussed later.

The second level of effect to be achieved is better eye contact and better reciprocal communication. Reciprocal communication refers to communication where a person asks a question or gives a statement and then pays attention to the response, and, hopefully, adds further to the conversation on the same or a similar topic. Patients with autism spectrum disorders talk "at" you. They tell you what they need, what they want, and what they know about. Often, they tell you more about what they are interested in than you want to hear.

The effects on reciprocal language should be of sufficient magnitude to be impressive to the family and may "proof" the diagnosis, if there has been some doubt as to whether the patient has an autism spectrum disorder or not. There are very few reasons, other than an autism spectrum disorder, why reciprocal conversation would be improved simply with the addition of an SSRI. One of the other disorders improved most commonly is elective mutism, and this disorder is often seen in patients that I am likely to end up giving a diagnosis of an autism spectrum disorder. The most successful patient I ever had in this category was a 4-year-old boy who only said "momma" and "no." After 4 months of taking fluoxetine (trade name Prozac), he sat on the exam table and told me quite a bit about the movie "Toy Story." I admit I've only had one patient who did that well, but I'm always hopeful I will see more. I have another 4-year-old boy who had such an improvement with fluoxetine that every relative he saw at Christmastime noted his improvement, and his dosage hasn't even been optimized yet. Finding the best possible dosage of a medication for a particular patient may require several months' time. Improvements in reciprocal language should be dramatic enough to be noticed by many people involved with the child, such as teachers, therapists, and relatives. It should not be an improvement so subtle that only the parents observe it.

There is a common adage that if the child with autism hasn't begun talking by the age of 7 years, he is not going to talk. I see this concern as a backward statistic. If the child is going to talk and have reciprocal language, he has usually done so by 4 to 7 years of age. If a child has not attained reciprocal language by age 7, it does not mean that I no longer attempt to achieve it, but the odds of building good, fluid language are much less than in the child who has developed some language by 4 or 5 years of age.

I believe that treatment with an SSRI medication creates the effects it does not by hooking up neurons in the brain to develop language, but, rather, it decreases anxiety, and anxiety is what has inhibited the development of reciprocal conversation. Children with delayed language and an autism spectrum disorder do not start speaking with baby talk. They seem to know how to talk—they just won't.

It would not be rare to see a child start talking after starting treatment with an SSRI medication and then lose that language after withdrawal of the medication. The language or increase in language does not have to revert, but, clinically, some reduction is often seen, unless the withdrawal of the medication is many months or years later. My medical model is that patients with autism spectrum disorders are born without enough serotonin effects in the brain. Since the SSRI only improves serotonin transmission while it is in effect in the body, then it is most likely that the patient is going to need to take the SSRI or something like it for the rest of his life. There is actually some medical evidence in adults that some improvement occurs in neuronal hookup owing to treatment with an SSRI, and this might mitigate a lifelong requirement for medication.

But, I have not seen it yet. When I prescribe a medication, I always let families know that the medications are most likely going to have to be taken long term to get the full benefit.

The third level of effect is to disinhibit the patient so he can, or will do, what others want him to do, such as schoolwork or homework. If the medicine disinhibits him too well, the patient doesn't care if he does his work or if he gets into trouble. This effect may cause a dilemma when it comes to deciding on the correct dosage for a patient who has autism or Asperger's syndrome. If the patient isn't doing his homework, is it because his anxiety level is increased and he's not taking enough SSRI medication? Or, is he taking too much, and he doesn't care if he does his work or gets into trouble?

Often, I have to alter the dose of the SSRI and observe the effects to decide if the patient is taking too much or not enough. If I raise the dosage of the SSRI medication, and the patient is even less likely to do his work or he sasses back more often to his parents and teachers, he is probably taking too much. If I lower the dose of the SSRI medication and his anxieties increase, which further interferes with his ability to focus and do his work, he is taking too little. Experience on the physician's part is very helpful in sorting out these types of issues.

It is important that when a medication dose is changed, either increased or decreased, adequate time must be given to allow the patient's body and mind to adjust to the medication change. How much time it takes to allow for adjustment varies with the medication, but most medications require about 2 weeks for adequate patient adjustment to a new dose. Some effects of the medications can continue to increase at the same dosage level over a period of 6 to 8 weeks.

I find it is fairly easy to accomplish a decrease in anxiety with SSRIs, and reciprocal conversation improves fairly easily with the right medication. Both improvements should be expected. Disinhibition, the ability to do what others want you to do, is much more difficult to achieve. In some cases, it just cannot be done. It is imperative that an attempt is made to achieve disinhibition, because a patient who is only willing to do what he wants to do is less likely to do well at school, at work, and in familial relationships.

One of the advantages of the long half-life of fluoxetine (trade name Prozac) is that it allows me to start dosing it less often than every day. It is common for me to start a patient on a dose that is taken Monday and Friday and then, after 3 weeks, increase the frequency of dosing to taking it Monday, Wednesday, and Friday. The advantage of the low initiation of dosing is that for a few patients, especially those with autism spectrum disorders, a dose twice a week is all they need. If I start a patient on a dose of fluoxetine every day, and he only needs it three times a week, there may be improvement at first, but then the level of the drug gets too high in the brain, and the effects are not as desirable. Also, if I start a patient on a dose that is taken Monday and Friday, and the family can tell that the patient is good on Mondays and Fridays, Tuesdays and Saturdays are not too bad, and the rest of the days stink, then they know it's the medication causing that effect, not that they were simply hoping it would work.

I have a preschool patient that I started on a dose of fluoxetine, taken twice a week. After 2 weeks, her mother reported that she hadn't wanted it to work, but it was obvious to her that it was. Escitalopram (trade name Lexapro) can be started on an alternate-day basis, but most of the other SSRIs must be started with daily dosing. Some will require dosing twice daily.

In a child, I will start the dosing of fluoxetine at about 1 mg per year of age, adjusted a bit if the child is overweight or underweight. When I see a new patient who has passed the age of 10 years, I will start with either 10 mg if he is closer to 10 years of age or 20 mg if he is closer to 20 years of age, with some adjustment for weight.

I conducted a study in the 1990s in which I looked at what dosage a group of my patients with autism spectrum disorders were taking after 1 year of medication treatment. The study included 88 patients, whom I had diagnosed with an autistic spectrum disorder during a 12-month period of time. After 1 year of taking medication, most of the patients who were taking fluoxetine (trade name Prozac) were taking 10 to 20 mg each day. There were nine who still took their fluoxetine less than every day, because that is all the medication they required for good results.

An interesting observation seen with fluoxetine is that if I am treating depression, I may have to wait 6 to 12 weeks to be certain the medication is not working. When I am treating anxiety in a patient who has autism or Asperger's syndrome, if I am anywhere close to the correct dose, I expect to see a difference with the first dose. Yes—the very first day! I often start a patient at a dosage level less than I expect to be the final dose, but, even then, it is not rare to see some effects with the first dose. Because I am looking for effects on day one, fluoxetine is given in the morning. It does not cause a patient to be tired, but it may help the patient sleep, if anxiety has been interfering with the patient's ability to sleep.

Fluoxetine has no direct effect on attention level. If a family returns and says the patient's attention level is better, I believe the anxiety was lessened, which was interfering with his ability to pay attention, rather than the fluoxetine having a direct effect on the patient's ADHD.

Fluoxetine is metabolized by a limited enzyme system in the liver (cytochrome P450, 2D6). This system also metabolizes other commonly used medications in the treatment of these patients. The professional must be experienced in using these medicines together, because a change made to one medication can actually affect two or three others that are being taken.

Sertraline (trade name Zoloft) is approved by the FDA for use in children 6 years of age and up. It has been shown to be effective, but it may take second place to fluoxetine, primarily because of its shorter half-life. Its half-life is significantly shorter than that of fluoxetine. In children, sertraline effects may not last an entire day. In a school-aged child, a low dose taken in the morning may not make it all the way to the end of school. In children, sertraline taken at low doses, such as 25 or 50 mg, may not last all day because it is being metabolized more rapidly than it would be in an adult. In a young patient, 25 mg taken twice a day may result in better effects than a single dose of 50 mg taken in the morning. Although the total daily dose is the same, the once-a-day dose may become ineffective in the evening, where the twice-daily dosing may well carry effects throughout the entire day. This is not a common problem in adults.

When I am using sertraline, I typically prescribe doses higher than 75 mg. I will start the patient at 25 or 50 mg, but I intend to get the dose to about 100 mg, and I expect that the dosage can be raised to that level over about a month's time. A dose of 50 mg of sertraline (trade name Zoloft) will work, but I do not believe it holds up well when a situation is encountered that is severely provoking to a patient's anxiety. Sertraline may have a little more "happy" to it than the other SSRIs do. I particularly like its effects in teenagers who are primarily being treated for anxiety but who also have a mild depression component.

Normal dosing of sertraline is between 50 and 200 mg taken each day. It does come in a liquid preparation, but the concentration is rather low, and it is used up quickly. The sertraline tablets are small, and most of my patients have been able to swallow them. In cases in which I am seeing no effects or poor effects with fluoxetine, sertraline is typically my next choice of SSRI to prescribe. If other family members have done well with sertraline, I am likely to start it initially. I am careful to ask about sexual side effects with sertraline. I don't often see sexual side effects in males, but I do see some in females.

Fluvoxamine (trade name Luvox) is not approved for use under the age of 18. Some studies have suggested that it may have a special place in the treatment of obsessive-compulsive disorder. My usage of fluvoxamine has been limited, but, so far, I have not found it to be a "first choice" medication in children.

I believe the SSRIs are better for alleviating and preventing anxiety than are the "benzos," or benzodiazepines (trade names Valium, Xanax, Klonopine, etc). The "benzos" are effective at relieving acute anxiety, but they are not that good at preventing it, unless they are taken regularly. Anxiety can also return quickly as the effects of the drug wear off. The "benzo" medications are addictive in nature and can lead to seizures, especially if the patient quits using them abruptly. There are some patients in whom the "benzos" have to be used, but, typically, they will be used along with an SSRI or an atypical antipsychotic medication. They are useful for infrequent, but known, high-anxiety situations.

I have a college-aged patient with Asperger's syndrome, who did well taking an SSRI and a stimulant medication, until he was standing in front of his speech class. At the podium, his sweating and rapid heart rate became so pronounced that he could not give his speech. One of the "benzo" medications, taken with his usual SSRI, worked well to get him through that class. A plane flight might also be a good time for usage of a "benzo."

I have one patient, a young woman with moderate Asperger's syndrome, who was supposed to take an international plane trip and could not tolerate the possibility of being touched during a search by the security official at the airport. She wanted me to write a letter saying that she could not be touched, owing to her autism. I told her that it would be best for me to try to lower her anxiety about an encounter with a security official by using one of these medications, as I did not believe it would be likely that she would be granted a medical release from a search at the airport, no matter what the reason. A dental visit might be another common usage for this type of medication. I do recommend that the patient try taking the medication at home prior to the appointment, because it is not rare that a patient with an autism spectrum disorder may respond in a manner opposite of what is typically expected.

It would be extremely rare for me to use "benzos" for the purpose of sleep initiation. They are somewhat effective, but they can be very psychologically addicting when used for this purpose, and, often, they just do not seem to work well in children, except on the first few nights of use.

There are also anti-anxiety, antidepressant medications, which affect both serotonin and norepinephrine transmission. The medications most commonly used today are venlafaxine (trade name Effexor) and duloxetine (trade name Cymbalta). There is also bupropion (trade name Wellbutrin), which is a dopamine and norepinephrine reuptake inhibitor. This group of medications is used primarily for anxiety and depression, but the norepinephrine effects may be helpful in a patient who has an autism spectrum disorder by improving social interest and the ability to read social cues.

There may even be positive effects on ADHD symptoms as a result of the increase in norepinephrine effects. These effects are very advantageous to the patient, as he deals with the world of typical development. The physician must understand that stimulant medications may also increase norepinephrine levels, and so, if the patient is taking both, the norepinephrine side effects must be watched for. When a patient is taking too much medication that stimulates norepinephrine, the main side effects are sweating, urinary hesitation (go to urinate and it won't start), and erectile dysfunction.

Bupropion may also lower the seizure threshold (make it easier to have a seizure) in patients who are susceptible to seizures. As I stated in an earlier chapter, patients with autism spectrum disorders have a higher incidence of seizures than that in typically developing youth or individuals with ADHD, so the use of bupropion in patients with autism spectrum disorders should not be undertaken lightly.

Occasionally, I will have a patient who benefits from an initial dose of an SSRI, but it does not provide enough improvement. When I subsequently increase the dose, there is either no further improvement, or there is actually a worsening of symptoms. At that point, the medication is typically changed to one of the other SSRIs. Again, improvement may be seen with the initial dose, but the improvement is not adequate, and a further increase brings negative results or no further improvement. Patients with this clinical picture may do best by taking low doses of two or three SSRIs rather than a large dose of any single medication. This is not common, and it doesn't make a lot of pharmacologic sense, but it has been my clinical observation.

When I do start a new SSRI with a patient, I do not usually stop the initial SSRI, but I will cross-taper them. Cross-tapering is achieved by not decreasing the dose of the initial medication until it has been shown that the patient is tolerating and benefiting from the new SSRI. Once the new medication is showing positive effects, the initial medication may be tapered away by lowering the dose over successive days or weeks. During the time of cross-tapering, there is also an opportunity to evaluate the effects of taking both medications at the same time.

Again, no one SSRI, at this time, is better than another. Some patients will simply respond better to one than another. How much the patient weighs or how bad his symptoms are does not tell me which medication will work the best or how much he will require. I always start low and go slow, but some patients will require a high dose. Especially with the SSRI medications, when one evaluates a patient's symptoms, too much and not enough medication may look very much alike. If a certain SSRI has worked well for a close biologic relative, assuming the child is not adopted, there is a good chance that medication will work well in the patient.

If I treat twins with similar diagnoses, I may start one child on one SSRI and the other child on a different medication. Whichever patient does better will indicate to me that they should both be prescribed the better medication. It is common within a family that each patient will be taking similar medications, although not necessarily the same dose. It is not common that one family member would take a very high dose, and the other family member a low dose, but some difference is frequently seen.

Taking SSRIs alone may lower the anxiety level around new social encounters, but they do not typically help with interest in social contact and reading social cues. The medications that also positively affect norepinephrine transmission are more likely to do that, in my opinion.

Once the SSRIs have gotten the anxiety under control and a stimulant is added, there may have to be an increase in the dose of the SSRI to compensate for the pressuring (worsening) of anxiety by the stimulant. It is not unusual in a patient with an autism spectrum disorder or a patient with ADHD and co-morbid anxiety to have to take an SSRI to be able to tolerate an adequate dose of a stimulant. Patients with ADHD and anxiety may tolerate an initial dose of a stimulant, but a further increase may raise the anxiety to an intolerable level, and an SSRI may have to be added. The stimulant medication may also have to be lessened or changed.

Once, I was relating to a colleague the results of the Multimodal Treatment Assessment study that had been published in 1999. This was a large landmark study funded by the National Institute of Mental Health. It had been shown in that study that children and adolescents who receive a diagnosis of ADHD are co-morbid for an anxiety disorder in 31% of cases and oppositional defiance disorder in 41% of cases. If one considers those patients who have received diagnoses of all three—ADHD, anxiety, and oppositional defiant disorder—I believe that many are not oppositional, but are adamant. That is, things must be the way they see it. In that group of patients, who have ADHD and anxiety and are adamant, I believe those patients may have Asperger's syndrome.

My colleague blew me off, stating, "Those kids are just weird!" A few years later, I had the opportunity to present the same concept again, and he responded, "Some of those kids have both—oppositional defiant disorder and Asperger's syndrome. You know, I think 20% of patients who come into our clinic now have Asperger's syndrome." I thought, "It is good that you understand."

Trying to break through the adamant behavior of these patients is a high priority for successful treatment. SSRIs often play a major role in decreasing adamancy, but they are often not fully effective. It can be difficult to correct being very adamant in some patients by taking only one SSRI medication, and it may be that augmentation with an atypical antipsychotic medication will be required.

SSRI medications are the main medication treatment used to lower anxiety in patients who have autism spectrum disorders. A wide variety of these medications is used, and finding the best possible medication and its best dose is accomplished slowly in most patients. Understanding the differences between too much and too little medication is important in achieving the best patient outcomes.

Chapter 7

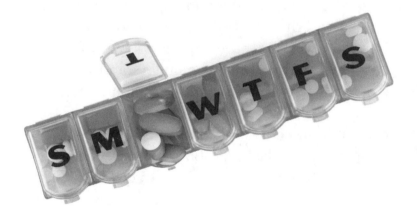

Atypical Antipsychotic Medications

If anxiety and/or depression cannot be controlled with an SSRI alone, then an atypical antipsychotic might have to be added. Antipsychotic medications are not as selective as SSRIs, which, for the most part, affect just serotonin. Antipsychotic medications affect many neurotransmitters to varying degrees. How much of each neurotransmitter is affected usually determines the differences in the effects between the medications within the group. These medications typically affect dopamine and serotonin, mostly decreasing the effects of these neurotransmitters, but they are sometimes used in combination with other medications that increase serotonin or dopamine levels. A typical example is when an atypical antipsychotic medication is given for aggression to lower dopamine effects, along with a stimulant for ADHD that increases dopamine effects. At this time, it is not known which neurotransmitters need the most adjustment in patients who have autism spectrum disorders.

Treatment of autism spectrum disorder with medications is based on affecting neurotransmitters that have been shown to improve issues in other disorders, such as anxiety, depression, and ADHD. Very few patients with higher levels of Asperger's syndrome will have enough symptoms to require the use of an atypical antipsychotic. However, there are exceptions. I have a patient who is now a college student. I have treated her since her early school days. She has moderately high-functioning Asperger's syndrome. For most of her school years, she has done well by taking a combination of atomoxetine (trade name Strattera) and sertraline (trade name Zoloft).

During her first year in college, she lived in a dormitory and made adequate grades, but she had some social issues with roommates. Her second year, she had moved off campus into an apartment with a friend from the dormitory. That roommate became ill and had to leave college in the middle of her first semester. My patient began having difficulty with going to class and doing her homework. She was concerned that she hadn't yet figured out what her major was going to be. She found it difficult to work on a subject that may end up not fitting into her major.

The addition of a small dose of aripiprazole (trade name Abilify) has improved her mood and self-confidence. She is now much more able to plan for classes, maintain her apartment, and do her schoolwork. The improvement in her demeanor has been noted by many others. She had been doing "okay" before the addition of aripiprazole, but she is really blossoming with the addition of this antipsychotic medication.

Typical antipsychotics are represented by medications such as haloperidol (trade name Haldol) and lithium carbonate. The atypical antipsychotics are a newer set of medications that hopefully have minimal side effects, particularly related to weight gain and potential for tardive dyskinesia, which is a movement disorder typically seen later in life in patients with certain psychiatric disorders and in patients treated with psychiatric medications, including atypical and typical antipsychotics. The group of atypical antipsychotics includes risperidone (trade name Risperdal) and aripiprazole (trade name Abilify), which are the only two medications approved by the FDA at this time for the treatment of autism spectrum disorders. These medications have been approved especially for the treatment of outbursts and aggression in autism spectrum disorders.

Quetiapine (trade name Seroquel), olanzapine (trade name Zyprexa), ziprasidone (trade name Geodon), asenapine (trade name Saphris), and clozapine (trade name Clozaril) are the currently approved atypical antipsychotics for use in adults, but more are in research or awaiting approval. These antipsychotic medications have been very helpful in patients with autism and Asperger's syndrome. They seem to help the SSRIs decrease anxiety; they stabilize mood, decrease outbursts and aggression, and may improve social interest and the ability to read social cues. Some of these effects are documented in double-blind controlled studies, and some are clinical observations.

Risperidone (trade name Risperdal) is one of the first atypical antipsychotics. It is now available in generic form and is an effective medication. It is FDA approved for use in autism for outbursts and aggression. It is not my primary "go to" medication when I use an atypical antipsychotic medication in patients with autism spectrum disorders. I believe that it must typically be given two to three times a day in children. This makes it a bit uneven during the day. Weight gain may be a problem, and this seems to be dose related. That is, the higher the dose, the more likely the patient will experience weight gain. Most weight gain seems to occur in the first year of treatment and then may plateau, if the dosage remains stable.

In some patients, risperidone increases levels of prolactin (a hormone), and this can result in breast enlargement and breast milk secretion in males and females. I typically try to keep doses below 6 mg per day, and many patients will do well taking a dose of 1 to 3 mg per day. While I tend to start with some of the other medications in this class, there are some patients who respond best to risperidone. If my back is up against the wall, particularly with outbursts and aggression, and I have not seen adequate improvements with another atypical antipsychotic medication, risperidone is the one I prescribe.

I have a patient who, when I first met him, seemed like he would achieve improvement easily. He was just starting elementary school. He was extremely bright and very verbal, with a large vocabulary. He could read and comprehend what he had read at about the third-grade level. His problems were with outbursts and aggression. He would get upset and hit other students and teachers. Although several antipsychotic medications were tried, he has ultimately done very well with risperidone, along with an SSRI and medications for ADHD. He now has fewer than two aggressive episodes in a semester. The outbursts are easier to defuse, and the reason for the incident has often resulted from being bullied or experiencing a major change of routine, such as having a substitute teacher who has not encountered this student in the past.

Quetiapine (Seroquel) is an effective antipsychotic medication, although the ideal dosage range may be very different for each patient. I know that most of my patients do best with a dosage in the 600- to 800-mg range, but there can be some effects even with 50 to 200 mg. Weight gain is almost always an issue and is related to dosage. The higher the dose given, the more likely there will be weight gain. In children, it often has to be given twice a day, while adults usually do well with a once-a-day regimen. Typically, the dose is started in the evening because sedation is common. This sedation may be helpful in the patient who has sleep initiation problems (trouble falling asleep once they have gone to bed), and I have seen it used just for sleep initiation. I do not typically use quetiapine just for sleep, because I feel it is better to try less costly sleep medications that have lower potential for serious long-term side effects.

Mirtazapine, clonidine, and melatonin might be early choices to use to treat difficulty with falling asleep, if a medication has to be used. They are not "true" sleeping medications, but they have the effects of making one sleepy. "True" sleeping medications like zolpidem (trade name Ambien) and eszopiclone (trade name Lunesta) and others have not been very effective in my patients who have autistic spectrum disorders. Not only might the medications not work well, but they may cause agitation and arousal. I definitely avoid using the "benzos" as a sleep medication as I mentioned previously, but, on occasion, they may have to be used. Medications used for sleep will be discussed in a later chapter.

Quetiapine might be started as low as 25 mg, but the dosage can be increased rather quickly, unless there is too much sedation. A dosage of 600 to 800 mg is the target amount, but a few patients are going to need even higher doses, usually indicated by the observation of a loss of

improvement or diminished improvement in behaviors achieved at a previous, lower dose.

Quetiapine (trade name Seroquel) may not
bind as tightly to receptors as the other atypical
antipsychotics, and some experts believe this
characteristic may decrease the potential for
long-term negative side effects. In recent years,
I tend to use the newer atypical antipsychotics
more than quetiapine, because they seem to be
a bit easier to dose and may have less of an issue
with weight gain. I must add, however, that I have
always been impressed with quetiapine and its
ability to improve reciprocal language in patients
with autism spectrum disorders.

I have had several patients do well on quetiapine. One illustrative patient has autism and has
very little language. He required that his mother
lay beside him in his bed to be able to fall asleep.
Should he awaken in the night and find that his
mother was no longer in his bed, he would begin
smearing feces around his bed and his room. In
this case, quetiapine was started first, because I
believed it may help him with sleep. However, he
had tried aripiprazole (trade name Abilify) in the
past to try and obtain language. His symptoms of
awakening and smearing feces have disappeared
after reaching a 400-mg dose of quetiapine. He

started by taking a lower dose, but his symptoms kept improving as the dose went up until, at 400 mg given in the evening, there was no longer a fecal smearing issue. He still requires his mother to be in his room for a while as he lies down, and there has been some improvement in language, but not as much as I often see in this population with the use of quetiapine. I used to believe that quetiapine helped children with autism be able to speak, and I still believe it does, but the other atypical antipsychotic medications are also capable of achieving that effect.

Olanzapine (trade name Zyprexa) is a very effective medication, but issues with weight gain and metabolic disorders, which may be worse in children compared with adults, make it less useful. It is now available in a generic form, which should help with cost. It does come in an orally disintegrating tablet, so it can be used even when the patient has trouble swallowing pills or capsules.

The weight gain issues with these products can be significant. I have seen a teenage male gain 19 pounds in 6 weeks' time, and he wasn't thin to begin with. When I am trying to determine if the medication is the cause of the weight gain, one of the main questions I will ask is whether the patient is up at night, foraging for food. If he is, then it is very likely that the medication is the cause of the weight gain, although I have had some patients who foraged for food at night and were not taking any of these medications.

Sometimes it gets very difficult to tell whether it is the medicine, a family trait, or the patient putting on some body fat that will go away as he hits his pubertal growth spurt. It is not rare to have difficulty deciding the cause in some patients, but, in most patients, the weight gain is rapid and immediate when it is due to one of these medications.

Checking the patient's height and weight at each visit and recording them on a growth chart is a good method to help determine if a certain medication has had an effect on weight. I have seen some patients in whom the weight gain was slow but persistent, and, after a couple of years, I could trace back down the growth chart and see that the increase started at about the time of the initiation of a certain medication.

If I determine that a certain medication is responsible for significant weight gain, I will try to discontinue it and substitute another medication that has fewer or hopefully no weight gain issues. Efforts to increase the frequency of exercise in a patient with an autism spectrum disorder have rarely been successful. I do have one patient, however, who walks 5 miles every day on a treadmill. I'm not sure how fast he walks, but exercise is helpful with maintaining his weight and reducing other symptoms.

Aripiprazole (trade name Abilify) is one of my favorite atypical antipsychotic medications at this time. It is almost always a once-a-day medication, is relatively easy to dose, and only has significant weight gain in about 15% of patients. When a patient does have weight gain secondary to taking this medication, it is almost always too severe to continue the medication, and the weight gain does not seem to be dosage related.

This means that a patient may gain weight even by taking 1 or 2 mg if he is susceptible to weight gain with aripiprazole. It is unfortunate when the medication is having very positive effects on behavior but I must discontinue it, owing to the weight gain. This medication is approved by the FDA for use in children and adolescents with autism spectrum disorders, and I have had several families who are so pleased with the positive effects that I hear, "I don't care what you're going to change, Dr Aull, but you're not taking him off of *that* one."

The changes seen with aripiprazole are improvements in anxiety and depression, evening of mood, fewer and less severe outbursts and aggression, more interest in social interaction, and improved reading of social cues. Side effects besides weight gain and mild initial sedation are dystonias and akathisia. These are movement disorders, such as tongue thrusting, a clenched fist that cannot be opened, or an odd twisting upward of the head and neck, and these are generally dose related. Children may be more susceptible to having dystonias than are adults. These movement disorders must be differentiated from tics and stereotypies, but, when observed, they will typically require a dosage reduction. However, I have found that many families are uninterested in continuing a medication that can cause such odd side effects.

Aripiprazole (trade name Abilify) is metabolized by the same enzyme system that also metabolizes several other psychiatric medications, and so it must be increased very slowly when the patient is taking one or more of the medications metabolized by this same system (cytochrome P450, 2D6). When aripiprazole was first on the market, I would raise the dose in 5- to 10-mg increments, but I now increase it much more slowly. One of the reasons for a slow increase is that aripiprazole builds in the system over several weeks' time and, therefore, it is somewhat easy to accumulate too large a dose. Most of my patients take 2.5 to 7.5 mg per day, but there are some who take 40 mg a day. Because the weight gain does not seem to be related to the dosage, the dosage can be increased, and an increase in weight as the dose increases is not typically seen.

Here is an example of the effects of this medication. I had a 17-year-old male patient whose mother was ready to kick him out of the house because of his behavior and sassiness. When he began taking aripiprazole at a dosage of 2.5 mg, a low dose for his size, he came outside and helped unload the groceries from the car, and his mother had not even asked him to do so. His mother was in shock over the result.

Another patient, who had moderate Asperger's syndrome, received a diagnosis at 12 years of age. He was treated with fluoxetine (trade name Prozac) and osmotic-release methylphenidate (trade name Concerta). He made reasonable grades, but he had trouble with outbursts and being critical of behaviors of other students. At 14, he was moved to an alternative school, but he exhibited similar issues. As he was about to be kicked out of that school, he began taking 2.5 mg of aripiprazole, with fantastic results. He became much more tolerant of the behaviors of others, and his grades also improved to "A's" and "B's." He scored 110% on a final exam. He became more socially confident and has not required an increase in dosage. He is gaining some weight, but he started that prior to the initiation of the aripiprazole. The patient and his family are so pleased with his success, they are working hard on diet and exercise to manage his weight.

I am not certain that I have ever seen this medication have zero effects in a patient. It almost always does something—maybe not what I wanted it to do, but it does something. If I find it truly has done nothing, I suspect that I may not have gotten the patient to a high enough dose to affect his behavior. I always tell the family what I expect a medication to do, and, together, we decide if it did it and subsequently adjust the dosing. Common goals in a patient with an autism spectrum disorder with the use of aripiprazole are increased reciprocal language, decreased aggression and outbursts, more even mood, less anxiety, less rapid frustration, and increased social interaction. I joke that aripiprazole should have an FDA indication for the treatment of being a complete jerk!

In the preteen and teen eras, it becomes difficult to tell if the cause of a certain behavior is adolescence, ADHD, anxiety, autism, or being antisocial. I call this the "A" phase. It is common that it is not clear which issue is at the forefront of the unwanted behavior, and a medication dosage change may have to be tried to help determine which behavioral issue is the most significant. Encountering a lot of patients with these disorders is very helpful with uncovering the correct diagnostic issue and treating it. Most parents are reasonably adept at noting improvements in behavior and attitude but are often cautious about using high doses or multiple medications with their child.

At this time, there is no single medication that treats the core deficits of autism spectrum disorders. Twenty years or so ago, the concept in most mental health areas was, "Let's see how much improvement can be achieved with the least amount of medication." Now the concept is, "Can I make it so most individuals don't know the patient has any problem at all, even if it requires multiple medications or a high a dose of a medication, within the scope of reasonable side effects and cost?"

A professional's experience is helpful when assessing whether more improvement may be obtained with any particular patient. I have seen enough patients over the years with various levels of autism spectrum disorders that I have a pretty good idea whether I should be able to get more improvement with medications or not, but there are times when the dosage has to be increased a little to ascertain whether more improvement may be achieved.

Asenapine (trade name Saphris) is a relatively new medication that is approved for use in adults with schizophrenia and bipolar disorders. The atypical antipsychotics are mostly used for treatment of bipolar disorders and schizophrenia, but there may be positive effects on symptoms of autism. As stated previously, risperidone and aripiprazole, both atypical antipsychotics, are the only medications that are FDA approved for treatment of autism.

Asenapine only comes in an orally dissolving tablet, and the bad taste of the original formulation can be an issue, but it is now available in a black cherry flavor, which is a major improvement according to patients I've treated. It comes in 5- and 10-mg orally dissolving tablets and is indicated for twice-daily dosing. I would say most of my patients do well with once-daily dosing. It is usually given in the evening, owing to mild sedation.

I have seen good effects with alleviating outbursts and aggression, and it is a common medication for me to change to, if the patient is gaining too much weight with another atypical antipsychotic. It is not without weight gain, but only about 15% of patients gain enough weight to make its continued use undesirable.

Effects are rapid and can usually be assessed after 1 week of taking the medication. I have not seen evidence of this medication having a significant buildup of effects over time. Therefore, I may raise the dose at 1- or 2-week intervals. I have been impressed that patients seem to be more aware of the effect of this medication than I typically see with other medications; therefore, they are willing to take it, in spite of the undesirable taste of the tablet.

After the pill has dissolved, the patient is not supposed to eat or drink anything for 10 minutes. Ingestion of a food or beverage immediately after the pill dissolves can lower the absorption of the dose. I tend to hear more complaints from patients about not being able to drink anything for 10 minutes than I do about the taste. It can also cause a numbing effect in the area of the mouth where it dissolves. This effect only lasts a few minutes and then disappears.

It would be nice to have a 2.5-mg tablet to use by itself or to be able to adjust the dosage between the 5- and the 10-mg doses. It does have some shared metabolic pathways with a few other psychiatric medications, and dosage must be watched if the patient is taking one of the other medications.

I have had several patients who have gained weight with aripiprazole (trade name Abilify) and who have not gained weight with asenapine (trade name Saphris), but there are some who gain weight with either medication.

I have one patient who is now at the college level. He has moderately severe Asperger's syndrome. When he first came to my office, he almost didn't make it into the office from the parking lot, owing to anxiety. He had been unable to attend school because of his anxieties about being around large or even small groups of people. He has tried several medications, but asenapine has given him the best results with the fewest side effects. He had responded well to aripiprazole, but he had a lot of weight gain while he took it. He did well with ziprasidone (trade name Geodon), but he developed significant dystonias, consisting of twisting of his head and neck. He actually felt that he was doing well and could tolerate the dystonias, but I discontinued the ziprasidone, and he has done very well with 15 mg of asenapine, without encountering dystonic movements.

I have a patient with moderate Asperger's syndrome who was very aggressive when I first evaluated him. He is a teenager. He had been recently dumped by his girlfriend of several months. He was convinced that she or even a stranger should be physically hurt to atone for his misery. He felt that inflicting physical harm on another person was justified by the emotional insult he had experienced. He is doing very well with asenapine (trade name Saphris), even though two other atypical antipsychotic medications had not worked for him. He is making good grades and now has plans to attend college. He is no longer aggressive.

Ziprasidone (trade name Geodon) is an atypical antipsychotic that rarely causes weight gain. I have only seen weight gain in a handful of patients, and I am always surprised when I see it. It might seem that without the weight gain, it would be the preferred antipsychotic to use. This is not the case, because it can be a bit more difficult to achieve the best possible dose in a patient than when using some of the other antipsychotic medications.

At low doses, those below 120 mg, it tends to be sedating. Above 120 mg, it tends to be activating. Although I routinely try to get a patient to a dose of at least 120 mg per day, it is not always clear who will need a further increase, and I have to resort to a trial-and-error method to see if a higher dose is beneficial. There is not an exact evaluation process for deciding how high an increase might need to be. Once again, start low and go slow with dosing, often in 40-mg increments, until the 120-mg-per-day dose is attained. Higher doses that I may decide to use are 160, 240, or 320 mg, although dosages higher than 160 mg per day are not FDA approved.

It is also a medication that exhibits a fair amount of dystonias. I believe it ultimately does have very nice effects on aggression, outbursts, reciprocal language, and maybe even social interests in patients with autism spectrum disorders. I do believe it is a little more difficult to tell if the patient is taking too much of this medication or not enough, compared with some of the other antipsychotic medications.

Ziprasidone (trade name Geodon) must always be taken with food, or there will be less than full absorption of the medication. I have had several families who have ceased giving it with food, because it was not bothering the patient's stomach. But that is not why it is given with food. When it is taken on an empty stomach, only 50% of that dose will be absorbed. It is important to repeatedly ask families how ziprasidone is being given, to be certain the maximum benefit is being attained. Most patients end up on ziprasidone owing to weight gain from taking the other antipsychotic medications, but I have had several patients who have done quite well with ziprasidone, resulting in better improvement than was seen by taking their prior medications.

Atypical antipsychotic medications are often very helpful with the treatment of symptoms in patients who have autism spectrum disorders. Usage of atypical antipsychotics should be undertaken with a physician who is experienced with their use. The potential side effects, especially long-term ones—such as weight gain and potential for tardive dyskinesia—are best assessed by a physician who has experience with the use of atypical antipsychotics, who can provide long-term follow-up.

ADHD

In most patients, once anxiety and outbursts are improved, ADHD is nearly always left to manage. The ADHD within autism spectrum disorders is not fundamentally different from ADHD alone, except that there are more potential causes of inattention. Every patient is different, and there are no hard rules as to which medication should be used. But, in general, especially in patients with an autism spectrum disorder, the side effects—rather than the direct effects—may dictate to a greater extent which medication is used.

Inattention in a patient with Asperger's syndrome may be caused by an inability to focus that is a result of ADHD, anxiety, or a learning disability. In patients with autism spectrum disorders, it is likely that the patient has difficulties with all three, often in varying degrees. Many studies have shown that medications have the greatest effect on the core symptoms of ADHD, but some of the stimulant medications have significant negative effects, especially in patients with autism spectrum disorders, such as worsening of anxiety or aggravation of social quietness.

The amphetamines, as a group, are considered to have the biggest effect size (amount of change in symptoms in patients in a group study) on the core symptoms of ADHD. This group includes mixed amphetamine salts (trade name Adderall), lisdexamfetamine (trade name Vyvanse), and dextroamphetamine sulfate (trade names Dexedrine and Dextrostat).

True amphetamines also have the most side effects. While the most prominent side effect is interference with appetite and sleep, the medications also pressure (worsen) anxiety, aggravate social quietness, and aggravate lack of tolerance of imperfection in others and sometimes in one-self. These negative effects are not limited to autistic spectrum disorders but are also seen in patients with ADHD and ADHD with co-morbid anxiety. The side effects on personality with these medications are typically dose related. This means that the greater the dose of the amphetamine compound, the greater the likelihood of negative effects. Age and level of school may be factors, also. A little social quietness is better tolerated, if needed to make good grades, during college than during middle school.

It is easier to adjust medication to minimize social side effects in college than in middle school or high school. In schools prior to college, a long-acting medication is most likely being used, because its effects are more even and there is no need to take a dose of medication at school. A patient in college may take a dose of immediate-release mixed amphetamine salts first thing in the morning for classes and not take another dose until after dinner to improve the ability to study. This schedule leaves the afternoon and early evening free of medication for social endeavors.

In general, mixed amphetamine salts (trade name Adderall) may also cause a patient to be quite "cranky" as it wears off. I advise patients to not call their girlfriends as they're coming off extended-release mixed amphetamine salts. They will likely get into trouble. These side effects may be eased with the use of an SSRI or an atypical antipsychotic. SSRIs and atypical antipsychotics are often used in patients who have an autism spectrum disorder for issues other than inattention, however. The atypical antipsychotics may also be used to counter the negative social and anxiety effects of stimulants in patients who have ADHD, although SSRIs are used more commonly. The atypical antipsychotic medications are not FDA approved to treat social side effects at this time.

In a patient who is already taking an SSRI or an atypical antipsychotic medication, a dosage adjustment—most often a mild increase—may be required after the addition of an amphetamine product to obtain the best overall results for the patient. In a patient who exhibits a lot of anxiety, I am unlikely to start treatment of ADHD with mixed amphetamine salts (trade name Adderall). I am more likely to pick another medication that typically exhibits less aggravation of anxiety. A physician cannot be certain that the negative side effects will be a problem for any particular patient until the amphetamine product has actually been given a trial. In general, however, the shorter-acting and less-even-release products aggravate anxiety to a greater degree than do the longer, more even preparations.

Dextroamphetamine salts (trade name Dexedrine) tend to have fewer negative effects on social interaction and less pressuring of anxiety than do mixed amphetamine salts (trade name Adderall). The time-release form uses a beaded technology for release. This is a system where half the beads will release quickly, and the other half will release their medication about 4 hours after the medication is first taken. This type of release system is a bit up and down when one looks at blood levels, direct effects, and side effects. These issues are not as bad as immediate-release medications, which must be taken about every 4 hours, but they can cause clinically notable problems in some patients.

I do like to use mixed amphetamine salts (trade name Adderall) for patients who are in college. Students who take a mixed amphetamine product will tell me, "If there is something that needs to be done, I cannot not do it." This medicine may make patients a bit obsessive about doing their work. But, those same students might tell me that they do not take their medication before a social engagement because they feel they are too quiet and don't participate in the fun as much as they would without their medication. I'm told, "I just sit there and watch others having fun."

It is appropriate for a patient to adjust his medication dosage for social reasons, once he is old enough to understand the positives and negatives of variable dosing. For normal dosing of mixed amphetamine salts, extended release (trade name Adderall XR) is 5 to 30 mg, and the immediate-release tablets are available from 5 to 30 mg.

I treated a patient who graduated from high school with a 3.2 grade-point average. She didn't do that well on tests, but she would get upgraded for her homework and in-class participation. In her first three semesters in college, she earned grade-point averages of 1.9, 1.7, and 1.4. College professors weren't that interested in homework and in-class participation. After starting treatment with mixed amphetamine salts (trade name Adderall), she achieved a 3.74 average and continued to do well, graduating with a 3.2, even after her poor semesters.

Although she had previously had some obsessive behaviors, such as eating one food at a time and using separate utensils, after starting to take the mixed amphetamine salts, she did become more obsessive. Sertraline was added to her treatment, which was effective in helping her with her anxiety and obsessive issues. In her case, I believe it was most likely the mixed amphetamine salts that gave her the ability to attain that high of a grade-point average.

She had previously received a diagnosis of dyslexia during high school, but I believe she had more of a short-term memory problem than true dyslexia. By the end of a sentence, she would forget what went on in the early part of the sentence. As a result, she would not have full comprehension. Clinically, a short-term memory deficit will appear like dyslexia, because it may result in poor reading comprehension. Because stimulant medications cannot improve true learning disabilities, except perhaps those tied to memory, her grade-point average should not have been able to improve as much as it did, if she truly had dyslexia. Dyslexia is a common co-morbid diagnosis in patients with ADHD.

I believe mixed amphetamine salts are a bit more effective in helping patients to get things in and out of memory than are the other ADHD medications. I believed this patient had to take mixed amphetamine salts (trade name Adderall) to be successful at school and that she had to take an SSRI to be able to tolerate the ADHD medication. Having to prescribe an SSRI to be able to tolerate an adequate dose of a stimulant is very common in patients with an autism spectrum disorder, although I do not believe this patient had an issue with autism. She more likely had ADHD and a co-morbid anxiety disorder.

Lisdexamfetamine (trade name Vyvanse) releases very evenly and lasts 13 to 16 hours.

Normal dosing is 20 to 70 mg a day in children and adolescents. It also eases off smoothly at the end of the day. The evenness of this medicine's effects, which is inherent to the processing of the medication within the body and is not an artificial release mechanism, minimizes side effects.

Because lisdexamfetamine (trade name Vyvanse) is so even, it is often considered a "first line" medication. I have been very pleased with this medication in patients who have autistic spectrum disorders. Many patients will tolerate it with only a slight increase in anxiety, and it tends to have minimal negative effects in terms of social interest and participation.

Its length of effect is a major positive attribute, because with other medications that are taken early in the day and wear off, issues with homework or tormenting of family members will frequently occur. In most cases, the higher the dose of medication given at the beginning of the day, the more obvious the effects when it wears off.

In the office, I am constantly trying to have family members note outbursts or meltdowns in terms of the time of day they happened and how much time had elapsed since the patient had taken his medication. It is not always easy for me to figure out which medication might be wearing off or if it could just be patient fatigue from the rigors of the day. It would not be uncommon for me to have to add a dose of a stimulant after school to help with maintaining attention in sports, driving, homework, or family relationships. Certainly, the 24-hour medications, such as atomoxetine (trade name Strattera) or long-acting guanfacine (trade name Intuniv), have an advantage in that they are not going to wear off in the afternoon. However, they may be getting a little weak by evening, if the child is dosed at bedtime.

It is very common for patients with an autism spectrum disorder to hold it together all day at school and then take it out on their families after they arrive home, because they know their families will still love them, no matter what their behavior. This issue is often anxiety driven, but it might be aggravated if a medication, especially a stimulant medication, is wearing off at the same time as the return home.

Methylphenidates come in short- and long-acting forms. Trade names are Ritalin, Ritalin LA, Concerta, Focalin, Focalin XR, Methylin, Daytrana, and Metadate CD. They are almost as potent as the true amphetamines but tend to have significantly fewer negative effects on appetite, sleep initiation, and social interaction. Normal dosing is from 5 to 72 mg with extended-release methylphenidate. Daytrana is methylphenidate in a transdermal patch, and normal dosing is 10 to 30 mg.

As a methylphenidate wears off, it is capable of creating emotional sensitivity in a patient. This sensitivity might be noted when a patient is more easily brought to tears and is less tolerant of correction or criticism as the medication ceases to be effective.

Two of the medications, trade names Metadate CD and Concerta, release a smaller dose in the morning and then a much larger dose about 4 hours later. Typically, this increase is tolerated well. With these medications, the professional must evaluate whether the morning dose is adequate to be able to maintain attention for the first 4 hours at school.

I typically see that if I give a dose adequate to last 11 or 12 hours with osmotic-release methylphenidate (trade name Concerta) or 8 or 9 hours with extended-release methylphenidate (trade name Metadate CD), then the immediate-release dose is adequate to cover the morning. I rarely "jump start" one of these medications with a short-acting methylphenidate (trade name Ritalin), because it may decrease the effectiveness of the afternoon dose. In certain situations, I will, but it will typically be a very early dose, where the child is aroused to take the medication and then allowed to go back to sleep for 30 to 60 minutes, and then the extended-release product is given as he or she goes out the door to school or to camp.

Transdermal methylphenidate (trade name Daytrana) produces effects that are very even. It begins to have effects evenly, and ends by having effects evenly. Effects last about 9 to 11 hours. Most of my patients who have used it like the medicine, owing to the very even effects.

The problem with this medication is that many patients with an autism spectrum disorder will not tolerate wearing a patch. It can also be a problem if the patient's skin will not tolerate the patch. I have one patient who does well on the patch because it can be removed, and the effects will stop in about 2 hours. This particular patient, who has moderate autism, only wears the patch for 4 hours.

Clinically, she seemed to be very slow at metabolizing methylphenidate products. Most of the other methylphenidate preparations would build up in her system, because she could not metabolize the entire dose in 24 hours. This would give her too high of an effect after several days or weeks of taking the product. The transdermal patch can be removed, and the methylphenidate effects will lessen in about 2 hours in most patients. It probably takes longer in this patient, but she is able to metabolize it adequately before taking her next dose.

Extended-release methylphenidate beaded-release (trade name Ritalin LA) and extended-release dexmethylphenidate (trade name Focalin XR) are beaded-release medications that release 50% of the full dose in the morning and the other 50% about 4 hours later. I tend to use a lot more of the extended-release dexmethylphenidate (trade name Focalin XR) rather than the beaded-release methylphenidate (trade names Ritalin LA and Metadate CD) because I believe it has fewer issues with aggravating anxiety and social quietness.

In studies, dexmethylphenidate extended release has been shown to have effects for up to 13 hours, but the effects are more potent in the first 8 or 9 hours, with a significant tapering of effects over the last 3 or 4 hours. Therefore, dexmethylphenidate extended release (trade name Focalin XR) is likely to last through the school day, but I will typically dose it twice daily, morning and after school, to cover homework, sports, driving, and family interaction. With dexmethylphenidate extended release, because the morning dose is not completely metabolized by the time school has ended, the late afternoon dose is generally smaller than the morning dose by about half. An afternoon medication would not have to be dosed every evening or afternoon if the situation does not require improved attention or if evening behavior is not a consistent problem.

I typically find that dexmethylphenidate has less interference with eating and sleeping than some of the other medications, so I tend to use it more often when an after-school or evening dose is required. Depending on the length of time needed for improved concentration or behavior, I will use either an immediate-release form or even a long-acting form, especially in an adolescent or an adult. Whether or not the patient is driving may be an important consideration when deciding whether to administer afternoon or evening medications.

Osmotic-release methylphenidate (trade name Concerta) works not by a beaded system but by a system of a capsule within a capsule that will not function correctly unless it is taken intact. This product must not be cut, chewed, or opened, or it will not work as intended.

In children and adolescents, I am rarely in favor of short-acting medications, because immediate-release methylphenidates will last from 2 to 5 hours and have to be administered at the school. I find it is best to avoid medication administration at school to avoid embarrassment to the child and the potential for medication dosing errors. Many patients feel singled out when they have to go to the nurse to take medications at school, although I have had patients with ADHD and autism spectrum disorders who enjoyed making the trip to see the nurse each day to get their medication. Children who are homeschooled could take the immediate-release medications more easily, but children and adolescents do not always do well with the up-and-down nature of the short-acting medications.

Children with ADHD and autism are also not good at remembering to take their afternoon medication. After all, if they could remember to take their medication, they wouldn't need it! Adults tolerate the short-acting stimulants far better than do children and adolescents. Adults seem to metabolize the medications more slowly, experience less "up and down" in focus and behavior, and are allowed to carry their medications with them. Adults also like to have the ability to fine-tune their medications to the course of their day. Most short-acting stimulants are available in a generic form, which will likely lower the patient's costs.

I am apt to start a methylphenidate product, rather than a true amphetamine, in a patient who seems to be getting along well socially. With methylphenidate products, I tend to see fewer negative social effects. This is not always true, and some patients will actually be more social when taking the true amphetamine, but it is not common. Also, the methylphenidates will typically aggravate anxiety to a lesser extent than will a true amphetamine, but I have seen just the opposite in a few patients.

I met with a family who brought in a fifth-grade girl that could not write a single sentence without a misspelled word. Her parents both had postgraduate degrees, and the patient had no history of head injury, neonatal issues, or meningitis. Her symptoms did not really meet DSM-IV criteria for ADHD, and the best I could surmise was that she had a problem related to the retrieval of information and short-term memory. In a patient with that kind of clinical picture, as discussed earlier, I am more likely to pick mixed amphetamine salts (trade name Adderall), and she began taking the timed-release form. She has made all "A's" ever since. She has noted a slight negative effect on her social interaction, which she is willing to tolerate.

Her brothers were so impressed with her improvement, they wanted treatment, as well! Her brothers did meet the DSM criteria for ADHD. The eldest was prescribed the same medication as his sister and did well. The younger brother, when I first met with him, had two friends and four enemies and was frequently getting into fights at the high school. I did not want to prescribe the mixed amphetamine salts (trade name Adderall) for him, fearing it would further aggravate his lack of tolerance for imperfection in others and make him more agitated or aggressive.

He began taking a methylphenidate extended-release product and, although he required a robust dose, his social issues improved. However, one day when he was out of his methylphenidate product, his mother gave him one of his siblings' mixed amphetamine salts. He went in to see a teacher to see what work he might be able do to catch up in that class, went right home, did it, and turned it in for credit. This improvement in recognizing a problem, seeking help, and following through until the paper was completed was so impressive, we switched him over to the mixed amphetamine salts product (trade name Adderall

XR). He did become more sullen and quiet, and he was eventually switched to lisdexamfetamine (trade name Vyvanse) and has subsequently done well in college. However, he does still require a robust dose.

This family illustrates that not all members of the same family will do well with the same medications. However, it is more common that they will. If I see siblings with the same diagnoses, I will often prescribe a different medication for each to see which sibling improves the most, and then give both patients the medication that has the best response.

It is typical that patients with autism spectrum disorders will not require as high a dose of a stimulant as do patients with an ADHD diagnosis without co-morbid anxiety or Asperger's syndrome. In fact, I tell other physicians that if they believe their patient is doing really well by taking the lowest doses of one of the stimulant medications, they need to at least consider whether a diagnosis of Asperger's syndrome might be a possibility. Most patients with an ADHD diagnosis will not do well with the very low dosages. As noted previously, it is possible that a patient with an autism spectrum disorder cannot tolerate as high a dose as that of a patient with just

ADHD, owing to the pressuring of anxiety by the medication.

When using stimulant medications to treat patients who have autism spectrum disorders, it is very important to watch mood, social activity, anxiety, obsessive behaviors, and irritability, along with the positive effects of the medications. It is important to ask the patient if he has noticed any negative effects, and it's important to ask if his friends have noted any differences and commented on or questioned the patient about behavioral changes. Questions like, "What's wrong with you?" or "Why are you doing homework at lunch?" or "Why are you so quiet?" or "Why aren't you going to join us at my house tomorrow?" are important to note.

Patients with autism spectrum disorders are often not very insightful when it comes to their own mood, so it is important to observe their behavior in the office and ask those who are around them about the patient's behavior. Stimulant medications can easily be responsible for an increase in anxiety, but the patient will usually be able to report that difficulty. He may not notice that he is less talkative, causing his friends to question whether he is depressed. He may become even more willing to stay home and play video games alone or maybe even study, meanwhile shunning social interaction. I am always asking patients if their girlfriend likes them better when they are taking or not taking their medication. I believe most patients are more attentive to their girlfriends when their medicine is working, but they may be funnier to her when they are not taking their ADHD medication.

Parents can be informative, but they don't always see the patient, especially an adolescent, in social situations. However, they may note that the patient is even less likely to join the family for dinner. Or, at dinner, they are even fussier about the poor table manners of a sibling or parent. They may become much more irritable and argumentative when corrected or asked to do something. Increased intolerance for imperfection in others is common in patients with autism spectrum disorders that are treated with stimulant medications.

I do not believe that severe depression is common in children and adolescents with autism spectrum disorders. However, ADHD medicines assist with attention and focus, and the medicine doesn't tell you what to focus on. If the patient focuses on what brings him down, he may get worse. I believe it is common to see an increase in social quietness, anxiety, and seriousness in patients who have autism spectrum disorders, and these symptoms may be easily interpreted as depression by others.

I have a patient with mild Asperger's syndrome who was pulled aside by several teachers to tell him that during the second semester of school, he seemed to have less focus in class and was participating less in class discussions. I am certain the teachers were concerned about depression, but I believe he was quieter because of his stimulant medication. However, his dosage had not been changed. His test scores were still very good, so I added a medication to take along with his stimulant, which should decrease his anxiety and improve his interest in social interaction. When I saw him in the office, I did not find any evidence of depression.

There are warnings about suicidal ideation with many of the ADHD medications, the SSRI medications, and the atypical antipsychotics. When I see suicidal ideation, I believe many patients with autism spectrum disorders are actually experiencing an increase in reciprocal conversation and are more likely to tell us what they have been thinking about. In my experience, a patient with Asperger's syndrome is somewhat likely to say that everything would be better if he wasn't living, but it seems to be fairly rare that he would act on it.

When asked directly about suicide in the office, patients with Asperger's syndrome are generally open in their discussion, and most have not thought deeply about how they would commit suicide. At times, I've had patients bring up suicide as if it were simply one of the alterative activities that could be done that day. Suicidal ideation is not to be ignored, and these patients should be watched closely. But, when I see them in my office, it is often clear that they are not severely depressed and do not have strong inclinations to die.

A patient I am treating is a teenager with Asperger's syndrome, and she was talking about suicide. When I asked what method she would use, she replied that she would get one of the guns that are used to shoot T-shirts into the stands at sporting events and shoot herself through the mouth. This is a rather absurd concept of a suicide method. It exhibits an unrealistic evaluation of a suicide attempt and, therefore, may be taken less seriously.

I am the most concerned when the patient has a carefully laid-out suicide plan. When the patient has a carefully laid-out plan, inpatient care is usually necessary. I am always a little more cautious with teenagers, preteens, and young adults when the reason for the suicidal ideation is a recent breakup with a girlfriend or boyfriend. I am also very concerned if the patient has a significant history of drug abuse.

In summary, stimulant medications are, and should be, used to alleviate ADHD symptoms in patients with autism spectrum disorders. I believe it is rare that a patient with an autism spectrum disorder is not going to require a medication directed at improving attention. The best possible dosing may be more difficult to achieve than it would be in a patient with simple ADHD. The social and anxiety effects of stimulant medications must be watched for and treated, if they are seen. Not all causes of inattention, especially in patients with autism spectrum disorders, are susceptible to ADHD medications.

Nonstimulants

The nonstimulant medications for ADHD are atomoxetine (trade name Strattera), extended-release guanfacine (trade name Intuniv), and extended-release clonidine (trade name Kapvay).

Their major advantage is their inherent length of action. They typically only need to be given once a day, although the extended-release clonidine is FDA approved for twice-a-day dosing.

These medications do not treat anxiety. They do not worsen anxiety, and they do not worsen social interaction. In fact, it is not uncommon to see improved social interest and reading of social cues with these medications in patients with an autism spectrum disorder.

Atomoxetine (trade name Strattera) seems to be almost tailor made for a patient with Asperger's syndrome. It helps with ADHD, doesn't worsen anxiety, helps with social interest and reading of social cues, and evens mood.

I have a patient who was prescribed atomoxetine when she was 16 years old, and she reported that she was the best she had ever been. She could read body language at school and at work, and the other girls accepted her better. Clearly, these effects were impressive, but that was not the only medication she took, and she had mild enough symptoms to where she was able to graduate from college with few academic accommodations.

This same patient complained at a later age that she could get a boyfriend, but she couldn't keep one. "My Asperger's is getting in my way."

She did tell a recent boyfriend about her Asperger's syndrome, and he commented, "That makes sense." The relationship continued several months more and ended only because she was leaving the country for an extended period of time.

Why do I not prescribe atomoxetine for all my patients? There are several reasons. I tell families that atomoxetine (trade name Strattera) is a "W" drug. It is either wonderful, or it is water. Atomoxetine works in about 60% of patients it is tried in. When it doesn't work, it generally does nothing.

It is a buildup drug, meaning it is going to take 6 to 8 weeks to be certain what the effects are at a specific dosage level. If I see a new patient toward the end of a school year who is in danger of retention, I usually have to use a stimulant to attain immediate effects. I must know within a few weeks if the patient's attention can be improved enough to convince everyone that his academic problems are related to his ADHD. Hopefully, he should improve enough with medication to avoid retention. After school lets out for summer break, I may decide to start treatment with atomoxetine during the summer.

Atomoxetine seems to have a fairly narrow ideal dosage range for each patient. The family must understand that it may take several months to attain the best possible dose. Then, the patient may grow and the dosage may have to be changed. Too high a dose of atomoxetine usually causes stomachaches (it should always be given with food), sleepiness (if a teenager is taking frequent naps, he is probably taking too much atomoxetine), sweating, urinary hesitation, and, in adults, erectile dysfunction. If the medication is taken in the evening, there tend to be slightly fewer side effects, and if it is taken in the morning, there tend to be slightly better direct effects.

The recommended dosage by the manufacturer is around 1.2 mg per kilogram of body weight, but I have found many patients who do well by taking less. A dose of 0.6 mg per kilogram of body weight is not uncommon in my patients who have an autism spectrum disorder, especially if they take another medication, such as fluoxetine (trade name Prozac), that inhibits the metabolism of atomoxetine.

I had a patient recently who has done well by taking atomoxetine once a day and fluoxetine three times a week. He seemed to be having a lot of recent issues with separation anxiety, and his fluoxetine dose was increased to dosing every day. His mother reported that he was sleepy in school and would take a nap when he got home.

She recognized that this effect was related to his dosage increase, and she returned him to his prior dose. It was not a direct effect of increasing the fluoxetine dose, but it was related to an atomoxetine dose increase that was secondary to the increase in the fluoxetine. I decided that he needed to switch from fluoxetine to sertraline (trade name Zoloft), partly because his father had done well with sertraline and partly so I could adjust the dose of his anti-anxiety medication without having metabolic effects on his atomoxetine.

On occasion, I have a patient who gets good social effects and ADHD effects at a dose level that also makes him a bit sleepy. In patients with this clinical picture, I may add a stimulant to help overcome the sleepiness. The use of two medications must be evaluated carefully, if for no other reason than the patient's cost. Atomoxetine is sometimes used along with a stimulant to cover the hours that are outside the stimulant's length of effect. This manner of dosing may also aid with issues related to a patient's sensitivity or tearfulness as a stimulant dose is wearing off.

Only the nonstimulants are still working in the morning. Some patients can get the whole house in an uproar before their stimulant medication begins to work. Families are typically very grateful for any improvement in a patient's behavior that may be obtained in the early morning prior to their stimulant medication becoming effective.

Guanfacine and clonidine have been used for ADHD for quite some time, although they were never FDA approved for improving symptoms of ADHD. Recently, with the development of newer, more even, longer-acting preparations, they have been FDA approved for use with ADHD.

Rapid frustration, hyperactivity, and impulsivity seem to be good therapeutic targets for these medications. The main side effect of these medications that limits their usefulness is sleepiness. Because these two medications were initially FDA approved for the treatment of high blood pressure, it is important that the dosage not be decreased acutely, as doing so may result in rebound headaches, dizziness, and hypertension.

Atomoxetine can be discontinued abruptly, and it will wean itself down, but clonidine (trade name Kapvay) and guanfacine (trade name Intuniv) should be tapered gradually at a rate of one dosage decrease per week. Intuniv and Kapvay are often used along with a stimulant medication for the treatment of ADHD. When they are used with a stimulant medication, the dosage levels of both medications are usually lower than when they are used alone.

Because they do not aggravate anxiety and stimulants do, it is possible to take a lower dose of a stimulant medication, along with clonidine or guanfacine. Being able to use a lower dose of a stimulant along with one of these medications in a patient with an autism spectrum disorder will usually achieve the same or better effectiveness with regard to attention, with fewer negative effects on anxiety and social interest.

Chapter 9

Sleep Issues

Many patients with autism spectrum disorders have sleep issues. The issues may concern sleep initiation (falling asleep), maintenance of sleep, and early awakening. Medications may be helpful for these issues, but it is seldom easy to find the correct medication treatment in patients who have autism spectrum disorders. Improvement of length and quality of sleep generally results in improvement in ADHD symptoms, anxiety, and mood.

Difficulty falling asleep can be anxiety driven, and, in those cases use of an SSRI medication for anxiety will likely improve sleep initiation. If there has not been improvement with the use of an SSRI, another therapy directed at initiating sleep may have to be prescribed. I generally use 45 minutes as a reasonable length of time to get to sleep after one has retired to bed. This does not, however, include any time lying in bed playing video games. If it is frequently taking 45 minutes or longer to get to sleep, I will prescribe a medication that will hopefully at least improve sleep initiation. This is usually not a "sleeping pill" but a medication that has sleepiness as a side effect.

Melatonin is one of my first choices of medication to improve sleep initiation. It has been studied in patients with autistic spectrum disorders and has been found to be effective. Dosing ranges from 0.5 to 10 mg, and it is taken in the evening, about 1 hour prior to bedtime. I have seen patients who fall asleep in 30 minutes after taking a 1-mg dose, but I have also seen patients who benefit little from taking 5 or 6 mg. In general, about a third of families that I meet with feel it works wonderfully, about a third feel it is helpful but not wonderful, and a third feel it is not effective. I do not know if some patients are just genetically less susceptible to its effects or if I never achieved the correct dosage level in those who saw little benefit.

Herbal products, such as melatonin, are not generally held to the same tolerances of dose that FDA-regulated medications are (meaning the contents of an herbal pill may vary greatly from pill to pill or capsule to capsule in terms of dose tolerance). If a family finds a melatonin product that is helpful, they should stay with that particular brand, even if it is a generic formulation.

I believe that melatonin is more helpful for sleep initiation than for maintenance of sleep, but there tends to be little issue with sleepiness causing difficulty awakening the next morning. There has been a study conducted in Europe, in patients with an autistic spectrum disorder, that showed improved maintenance of sleep when an extended-release melatonin was used. I have used the extended-release products, which seem to be more difficult to find at this time, and I again see one third of my patients do very well, one third do moderately well, and one third have poor effects.

Clonidine, a blood pressure medication, has a long history of use in helping with sleep initiation. I have found it fairly effective in many patients, and it seems to cause no "hangover" or sleepiness in the morning. It only lasts about 4 hours, and there may be nighttime awakening as it wears off. Usual dosing is 0.1 or 0.2 mg, given about a half hour before bedtime. I am very reluctant to go much higher than 0.3 mg because of its effects on blood pressure, which may cause difficulty with dizziness or fainting. I typically see better mood in patients who have been using clonidine, but I believe that is due to a better night's sleep rather than a direct effect of the clonidine on mood. Clonidine should have long worn off by the morning. This is not the long-acting product (trade name Kapvay), which is released over a longer period of time and, therefore, causes less drowsiness.

Guanfacine is a related medication that may also cause sedation, but it is more long lasting than clonidine. It is probably not as good at improving sleep initiation as clonidine, but it may be more helpful than clonidine at maintaining sleep. I have known physicians who recommend giving clonidine and guanfacine together to improve sleep initiation and maintenance, but I have not used that dosing with any frequency. Doses of guanfacine are typically 1 to 3 mg and are given at bedtime.

The new extended-release guanfacine (trade name Intuniv) may be a help for sleep maintenance, but it is not yet clear whether it is more effective for sleep if it is given in the morning or the evening. Short-acting clonidine and guanfacine should not be given along with the longer-acting preparations (trade names Intuniv and Kapvay).

Mirtazapine (trade name Remeron) is an antidepressant and anti-anxiety medication that has significant side effects of increased sleepiness and appetite. The increased sleepiness effect is frequently strong enough to help with both sleep initiation and maintenance. Since it is also helpful with appetite and anxiety, it is a medication I use frequently in patients with autism spectrum disorders, especially if they encounter decreased appetite or increased anxiety with a stimulant medication.

It also comes in an orally dissolving tablet, which may be more effective for sleep initiation than the regular tablet, but it does have an unpleasant taste, especially in generic form, that some patients will not tolerate. It is available in a regular tablet, which has fewer taste issues, and both the tablet and the dissolving tablet are usually dosed from 7.5 to 45 mg.

It is given about 30 to 60 minutes before bedtime. It does help with sleep maintenance, but too high a dose will result in sleepiness in the morning or difficulty with morning arousal. It may allow deep enough sleep that enuresis (wetting the bed) may be a side effect. Mirtazapine is generally well tolerated and very even in its effects. At the proper dosage level, it should not cause sleepiness during school hours.

Quetiapine (trade name Seroquel) is an atypical antipsychotic that is used for sleep initiation and maintenance. When using it for sleep, the dosing is usually 25 to 200 mg, and it helps with both sleep initiation and maintenance. Too high a dose will generally cause sleepiness in the morning. I do not regularly use quetiapine for sleep, unless I also need it to help with treating anxiety, outbursts, or aggression in a particular patient. In patients that need it for those reasons, the dose will usually be much higher than 200 mg. Cost and potential for long-term side effects are also serious concerns about its use only as a sleep aid.

Ziprasidone (trade name Geodon) is another atypical antipsychotic that has significant sedative side effects, at least at lower doses, such as less than 120 mg. Low doses given at night may be helpful for sleep initiation and maintenance, but doses used to treat anxiety and aggression tend to be at least 120 mg and higher. It is possible to prescribe the medication with a higher dose in the morning and a lower dose in the evening to try to get sedative effects to help with sleep but still have good effects during the day to help with anxiety and aggression. Again, cost and long-term side effects are concerns, unless the ziprasidone is also needed for other reasons, such as aggression or anxiety.

Some of the older tricyclic antidepressants, such as imipramine, desipramine, and clomipramine, have sedating effects and may be helpful for improving sleep maintenance. These medications are also helpful for anxiety, depression, and ADHD. They are useful medications, but they are not as specific in their effects as the newer SSRIs, and, taken in overdose, they may be fatal. I tend to not use them when there are small children in the patient's household, who might take an accidental overdose.

Triazolopyridine (trade name Trazodone) is an antidepressant medication that is unrelated to the tricyclic and SSRI antidepressants. It has significant sedative effects and can be useful for sleep initiation and maintenance. It fortunately does not have a lot of other side effects and is usually dosed in the 50- to 150-mg range, about an hour before bedtime. I have some patients who have done very well with triazolopyridine, but others have not, at least over a prolonged period of time.

Diphenhydramine (trade name Benadryl) and other antihistamines have been used for sleep initiation for many years, although recent double-blind controlled studies have not reported great success when used for this purpose. Many patients I have treated have had at least partial successes with this medication. Dosing is in the 12.5- to 50-mg range, adjusted for weight. Other antihistamines, such as hydroxyzine (trade names Atarax and Vistaril), may be somewhat more potent in their sedative properties and can be very helpful for sleep initiation, but they may not continue to work well over a prolonged time with regular usage.

Chapter

10

Treatment Examples

A patient with very mild Asperger's syndrome may well need to start on treatment aimed only at ADHD. If one is going to treat a patient with Asperger's syndrome solely with an ADHD medication, it makes the best sense to start with a medication that might have the least negative effects on anxiety and perhaps start with one of shorter duration until effects can be evaluated. Any stimulant should first be given a trial on the weekend or during a school break and then added on school days if there have not been significant negative effects on anxiety, appetite, or sleep. One cannot evaluate the medication's effects on school performance when the patient is at home, but if the patient is a wreck at home, it is highly unlikely he would do well at school when taking that medicine or that particular dose.

In a patient with an autism spectrum disorder who is only going to be treated for ADHD, atomoxetine (trade name Strattera) may hold a special place. Dexmethylphenidate (trade name Focalin) and lisdexamfetamine (trade name Vyvanse) may also be good choices, but they should be started at one of the lower available doses. At lower doses of these particular medications, there seems to be little aggravation of anxiety in patients with mild autism-related symptoms.

Patients with moderately high-functioning and high-functioning Asperger's syndrome may easily get by with treatment of ADHD alone, if there is little anxiety. However, I am always asking questions about anxiety symptoms and social issues when the patients return for follow up. A patient who has moderately low-functioning or moderate Asperger's syndrome is most likely going to have enough issues related to anxiety that medication directed at anxiety will be the initial treatment. In patients in these categories, the anxiety is impairing enough that it must be dealt with first, not just for improvement, but because any anxiety will almost always be aggravated with any amount of a stimulant medication given.

With a patient in this category, I might start with fluoxetine (trade name Prozac) at about a 1-mg dose per year of age. In other words, a patient the size of a 10-year-old would start at 10 mg. I also tend to start treatment with fluoxetine by giving it only on Monday and Friday for 3 weeks, and then the dose is increased to Monday, Wednesday, and Friday, unless the patient has greatly improved, which does indeed happen on occasion.

The family is instructed to call the office within 2 weeks or sooner if there are negative effects, and then the patient will be seen again in 6 weeks. At the follow-up visit, the patient will be evaluated for effects and side effects, and it will be noted whether family members can tell the difference between the days the fluoxetine is given and when it is not. If the family believes the anxiety is markedly improved and they cannot tell the difference between dosing days and non-dosing days, then a treatment directed at ADHD is initiated.

It would be uncommon to achieve adequate improvement quickly. More often, the fluoxetine dosage would be increased, and the patient would be asked to return in about 2 months. If there has been little effect after the first 2 weeks, then the dose will likely be doubled and increased to three times a week. If there is a fair amount of improvement, then the dose may be doubled by giving the same dose 6 days a week. Seven days a week is easier to remember, but if the family can still see a difference in the patient's behavior on the day when the fluoxetine is not given from that of the other days, then the dose is probably still a little low.

Fluoxetine does not always have to be given at the same dose every day, because of its long half-life. If I am trying to achieve a dose of 30 mg a day, fluoxetine isn't available in a 30-mg tablet or capsule, so I will prescribe 20 mg to be taken every other day and 40 mg to be taken on alternate days. If the family can tell that the 40-mg day is better than the 20-mg day, then I know the dosage needs to be increased. Once I believe the fluoxetine is close to the correct dosage, then medication can be started that is directed at the ADHD symptoms, while recognizing that there may have to be further adjustment of the fluoxetine after the initiation of a stimulant medication.

Here is an example. I was treating a boy who was in elementary school. His father related that prior to his son taking fluoxetine, when he picked his son up at school, there would be a group of boys standing together, and his son would be standing alone further down the sidewalk. After taking fluoxetine, his son was not only waiting with the group, but he was not always standing with the same boy within the group.

I was treating a patient many years ago, whose father was interviewed on television about his daughter who has autism. During the interview, he stated that he knew that 30 years from now, they may find something harmful about giving his preteen daughter fluoxetine, but, at the time, the medication allowed him to be able to take his daughter to the park with her sister, so he was going to keep giving it to her. He couldn't take her to the park before starting her treatment with fluoxetine, because of her anxieties and fears. Fluoxetine has since been shown to be safe and effective and is FDA approved for use in children of 6 years and older.

If I prescribe sertraline (trade name Zoloft), it must be given every day, and I have a certain dosage range to attain. I will usually start at a dose of 25 to 50 mg, depending on the patient's size, and try to work my way up to a dose in the 100- to 200-mg range. Dosage is usually increased weekly, but there may be some periods when a dosage level is held steady for a few weeks and subsequently increased. If 150 mg of sertraline works better than 100 mg, and 200 mg works better than 150 mg, I may give 250 or 300 mg a trial, although these are above FDA-recommended dosage levels. One must remember that because of the more rapid metabolism in youth, doses such as 25 or 50 mg may not last all day in a preteen or a child.

Too much fluoxetine (trade name Prozac) or sertraline (trade name Zoloft) leads to too much disinhibition and an "I don't care" attitude. A parent might hear, "I don't care if I do my homework," "I don't care if I get in trouble," or "I don't care if I smart-mouth back at the principal."

Escitalopram (trade name Lexapro) or citalopram (trade name Celexa) is often used if there has been poor success with fluoxetine or sertraline, but it can also be used if there is a family history of the successful use of that medication in a relative. It may be dosed initially on alternate days and is usually administered in the morning. Normal dosing is 10 and 20 mg, but it would not be unusual to have to go a little higher. Going higher, however, is not FDA approved. I find the effects to be more consistent in adults and teens than in young children, but there are some patients for whom it works quite well. Although it has a low incidence of side effects, sexual side effects are not rare in adults.

Bupropion (trade name Wellbutrin) has been a good medication to use in patients with an autism spectrum disorder because it has positive effects on anxiety, ADHD, and mood. It helps with weight loss and quitting cigarette smoking. It is a first-line medication if there is a strong family history of bipolar disorder or if it is uncertain if the diagnosis is bipolar disorder or Asperger's syndrome.

There is concern that bupropion may lower the seizure threshold in patients who are susceptible to seizures, and that issue may make one cautious about its use. There is a lower incidence of seizures if the dosage can be kept below 450 mg and if a longer-acting form is used. I usually use the bupropion XL dosing formulation, which lasts at least 24 hours in most patients.

The ADHD effects of bupropion have been described as being as effective as methylphenidate (trade name Ritalin), but I believe it is not that potent in most patients. It is a medication that may allow single-medication dosing that will treat anxiety and ADHD. It may also have a positive effect on social interest and the reading of social cues. If I prescribe bupropion and there is evidence that the patient experienced a seizure, I will discontinue the bupropion, chalk up the seizure to the medication usage, and do no further seizure workup unless the seizure is severe, long lasting, or repeated.

The group of patients with lower-functioning Asperger's syndrome and higher-functioning autism may often require the addition of an atypical antipsychotic medication. The most common reasons for their use are to augment an SSRI to lessen anxiety and to decrease outbursts and aggression. Atypical antipsychotics would rarely be a first-line medication, except for treatment in the very aggressive or self-injurious patient, which is more typical of a patient with classic autism.

I believe that the atypical antipsychotics are better at helping an SSRI treat anxiety, rather than using the antipsychotic, by itself, to treat the anxiety. Typically, I would not use an atypical antipsychotic medication to treat anxiety until several trials of different SSRIs had been attempted and were found to result in inadequate improvement. The SSRIs carry less concern about long-term side effects than do the atypical antipsychotics, and they often work quite well for anxiety.

In patients with classic forms of autism, atypical antipsychotics are more likely to be used and are used earlier in the course of treatment. I still tend to begin with the SSRIs in patients with moderate and severe autism, but I'm quicker to use the antipsychotics to assist with outbursts and aggression in those patients. I believe that the more improvement I can accomplish with an SSRI, the lower the dosage of an atypical antipsychotic I will need to use.

The atypical antipsychotics seem to be more helpful than the SSRIs for improving reciprocal language in the more severely affected patients. Patients with classic autism are most likely going to end up taking an SSRI, an atypical antipsychotic, an ADHD medication, and perhaps a medication to improve sleep.

In summary, many medications are used to treat the symptoms of autism and Asperger's syndrome. It requires experience on the part of the professional to know when and why a certain medication should be used or discontinued.

Tenets of Treatment

It is important to have a goal for any medication used. What do I expect the medication to do for this patient? What am I trying to correct? How do I and the family assess the effects? Sometimes, the goal is better grades. That's easy. One has numerical or alphabetic evaluations that can be followed over time. But, even grades don't always give a clear picture. Maybe the student gets the "A" because it's his favorite subject, or maybe he always struggles in math, or maybe he likes that teacher, or maybe his girlfriend is in that class, thereby setting up a competition to get the best grade.

I had a patient with ADHD whom I thought was appropriately medicated, but he would get a mix of high and moderate grades. For his 16th birthday, his father got him a somewhat high-end, brand-new, fast luxury car. My patient's mother was not pleased, but, of course, the patient was. He immediately wanted to add an aftermarket rear wing to the trunk lid, which would significantly decrease the value of the new car.

I suggested a deal. If he maintained straight "A's" by the end of the semester, he would be allowed to get the wing. His parents agreed. Lo and behold, he got all "A's." So, if the parents or I can find a good enough "carrot," the "carrot" can be a motivator for getting good grades. The family will just have to keep finding new ones. Long-term planning is often poor in patients who have an autism spectrum disorder; however, even with an appropriate "carrot," not all patients are going to be able to improve their performance.

If things are not going well with medication, it is almost always one of the three "D's." The three "D's" are wrong *drug*, wrong *dose*, and wrong *diagnosis*. As I talk with others in the field of psychiatry and behavioral pediatrics, it is amazing how often one will hear that the referring physician assigned the correct diagnosis and prescribed a good medication. All the psychiatrist or behavioral pediatrician has to do is increase the dose of the medication already initiated to achieve the desired outcome, such as lowered anxiety.

I commonly see patients with mild forms of Asperger's syndrome who have received a diagnosis of only ADHD. Their improvement will depend on receiving treatments and accommodations that are appropriate to Asperger's syndrome, not just changes in their ADHD medications. However, this may be one part of the adjustments made. The wrong dose of a medication may result in too little effect or too many side effects. Side effects could be related to too much or too little medication. The wrong medication may also give little effect or too much side effect. This issue is probably the most difficult to evaluate, particularly if the patient is taking multiple medications. Rarely, all medications will have to be stopped and the entire treatment process started over.

The milder the patient's symptoms, the easier it should be to improve the clinical situation. Some family members, and even some professionals, believe that if the patient's symptoms are very mild, he doesn't require medication. But, these patients might readily benefit from taking medication, perhaps even more so than the patient who has more severe issues.

I also see patients whose verbal skills seem to be so good at the initial exam that the severity of their disorder goes unrecognized for a while. Ultimately, they may end up taking more medications or higher doses than might have been anticipated originally. It is important to continually reevaluate any patient who is not doing as well as expected in relation to his particular diagnosis and severity.

In autistic spectrum disorders, taking too much medicine or not enough medicine often look alike, but not for the same reasons. For example, if a patient is having trouble paying attention, and his ADHD medication dosage is increased, if he is not improving, it may not be the direct effect of the medication. It could be that the patient's anxiety level has been raised, and he is unable to focus. It could easily be interpreted that his medicine dosage needs to be increased further, but this would likely increase his anxiety, therefore impairing his ability to pay attention even more.

The ultimate goal of treatment with medication is to effect enough improvement so that most individuals do not know the patient has any problems at all. This is not always achievable, but it is the goal.

Reciprocal conversation is a major goal. If a patient's parents are no longer living, the patient will do the best in the long term if he has good reciprocal conversation. Success at school, and, hopefully, a diploma and an employable skill are reasonable goals that can frequently be obtained.

Learning how to drive and then driving alone are major goals. Many of my patients are capable of driving. They are not adventurous drivers, and often they do not ask to be taught or to be allowed to drive. They tend to be cautious drivers, not road racers like my patients with ADHD, although they may have trouble with the unwritten rules of the road.

I had a patient who came to a four-way stop at a busy intersection at rush hour. The car across from him came through the intersection. My patient decided it was his turn and was almost hit on both sides by the cars to his right and left. Those drivers had assumed that, if he was proceeding through the intersection, he would have gone at the same time as the person across from him. My patient did not understand this unwritten rule.

I have a patient who finally got his driver's license during his senior year in high school. He would mostly just drive to and from school.

But, one day, he got on the Internet and found directions to a college about an hour away from home. He decided to drive there and visit it by himself. I was very pleased and thought this was a good sign that he was ready to go off to college. However, his anxiety got the best of him, and he returned home after spending just a few weeks away at school. He stated that he wasn't ready for college.

Treatment with SSRI medications may expose ADHD. I have many patients for whom I prescribe an SSRI to lower their anxiety, and it seems that their ADHD gets worse. In situations such as this, often the anxiety is keeping the rule-governed behavior in check, and, as the anxiety level is lowered, they appear more impulsive or are more likely to break rules or get into trouble. This should be expected as a result of treatment, and it means that the ADHD is going to have to be treated once the anxiety is under control.

Treatment of the ADHD with a stimulant medication may increase the patient's anxiety level, and a seesawing of the dosages of each medication may ensue before ultimately reaching the optimum effects on both the ADHD and the anxiety. I have had patients who, after their anxiety had been lessened, might "borrow" money from their parent's wallet to buy something small that they want. When they got caught, they were disinhibited about getting in trouble. But, this behavior may also be seen in typically developing children.

I was talking with a child psychiatrist several years ago, and it was clear that what I considered disinhibition as a result of using an SSRI, he considered hypomania (a state of extreme elation, often associated with bipolar disorders). The difference in the two diagnoses takes the physician down very different medication pathways.

Stimulant medications can pressure anxieties. This doesn't mean they cannot be used—it just means they must be used with care, and the patient's anxiety level may have to be controlled, usually with an SSRI, so the patient can tolerate taking an adequate dose or even any dose of a stimulant.

Patients with autism spectrum disorders are often very sensitive to even very small changes in dosing. What might be considered a small increase may cause effects as if the medication dosage were doubled. Obviously, start low, go slow, and try to only change one medication treatment at a time. Stopping one drug and starting another is not doing one thing at a time—it is doing two things.

Treatment with stimulant medication may aggravate social quietness, pressure anxiety, and aggravate a lack of tolerance for imperfection in other people and sometimes in oneself, especially in patients who have autistic spectrum disorders, but also in patients with ADHD. Medications that increase the effects of norepinephrine may help with social interest and the reading of social cues in patients who have autism spectrum disorders.

I have observed that patients with an autism spectrum disorder seem to always have three problems in dealing with life: failing to plan, failing to understand that they fail to understand, and failing to understand that what they do today will have an effect pertinent to a later outcome. These three issues are very upsetting to parents and spouses.

A high level of verbal skills may mask the severity of the disorder. I have seen a few patients whose vocabulary and use of language seem so good that I believe their problems should be easy to fix. But, as treatment is started, improvement does not come as readily as I had initially expected. This type of patient may be one who well meets the criteria for Asperger's syndrome but ends up taking an atypical antipsychotic medication to control meltdowns or outbursts and aggression.

Most children who have an autism spectrum disorder are visual learners. If they cannot picture what they are reading, it may be difficult for them to understand and remember what they just read. Anything that can be done to help them "picture" the written word should improve their academics.

The first and second grades mostly involve rote learning, and children with an autistic spectrum disorder may do very well, at least with the academics—perhaps not with social skills and following directions. Telling a student that, "You may want to take your math book home this weekend in case there is a test Monday," does not make it clear to a child with an autistic spectrum disorder that there will be a test on Monday. A child with ADHD may be more likely to stand out at the first-grade level as having difficulties than will a child with Asperger's syndrome.

The third grade consists of giving a lot more directions to be able to complete a series of tasks, such as "finish this or that before lunch or the end of school." In the third grade, patients with ADHD and autistic spectrum disorders will have more trouble with following those directions and being efficient about carrying them out.

Patients with autism and Asperger's syndrome typically loathe homework. School is for schoolwork, and home is for eating, sleeping, watching TV, and playing video games.

Fourth grade represents the major shift away from show-and-tell learning to learning by means of lecturing and reading. This change in how concepts are taught now hits on learning disabilities that are related to reading comprehension and auditory processing. Children who cannot read well also commonly take poor lecture notes. Patients who have autism spectrum disorders often experience great difficulty with picking out the most salient points in a chapter or a lecture.

By the time middle school arrives, everyone is having difficulty, but, for the patient with an autism spectrum disorder, directions, questions, and answers are more abstract in nature and are more difficult to understand. Test questions are not asked in the same manner as they were presented. Middle school also adds social issues to the mix, which are a problem in autism by definition. But, this will happen to varying degrees. Patients with milder forms of autism spectrum disorders are often bullied in middle school, especially between classes, during lunch and gym, and on the bus.

Generally speaking, autism and Asperger's syndrome are tolerated better by peers in high school and college, although maybe not with regard to dating.

In college, the skills of a student with Asperger's syndrome can be revered. When I was in college, I knew a student who lived down the hallway who was majoring in physics. His nickname was "The Fox," because he was so quiet and so smart. I saw him play chess against three very good players. They sat in one room with the board and would together decide on the best chess move. They would then call The Fox on the phone and tell him what move they had made. He did not have a chessboard in his room. But, he could picture the move in his mind and was able to keep track of the game in his head! He beat them repeatedly. He had one date in high school and moved in with a girl in graduate school. I do not know how he turned out, but I am certain that today I would diagnose his traits as Asperger's syndrome.

Most employment is lost because of coworker and management relationship issues. It is not because the patient cannot do the work or because he cannot arrive at work on time. I had a patient who would arrive at work 1 hour early and then go to the employee room and take a 20-minute nap. He had not clocked in yet. A new manager arrived and was ready to fire him for sleeping in the employee room. In this particular case, I was able to talk to the personnel in higher management, and the employee was allowed to stay.

Many patients will do well at school and then come home with the attitude that, "I held it together all day, and now you're going to get it, because you'll still love me afterward." The family may see acting out or aggressiveness toward siblings and parents that would never be seen in school or out in public. This behavior can lead to a consideration of an oppositional defiant disorder.

In Closing

I hope this book has given families the information they need about how medications might be helpful for some of the symptoms of autism spectrum disorders. I have done my best to explain how medications might have positive and negative effects and why. It will ultimately be up to the physician or other healthcare professional to sort out what is causing which symptom and why. Experience with the treatment of autism spectrum disorders will be helpful with the evaluation of symptoms and behaviors.

I would also like to take this opportunity to relate to you my "Four Rules of Life" that I believe all children should understand before reaching adulthood.

Dr Aull's Four Rules of Life

Rule 1: "Life isn't always fair." This is a simple rule, but it is often complained about by children.

Rule 2: "RHIP" is a military acronym for "Rank Has Its Privileges." This is why older siblings get to stay up longer than the younger ones. This is a rule that will be challenged by both children and adolescents.

Rule 3: "He who has the gold makes the rules." Parents have the gold; therefore, they get to make the rules. This rule is also challenged often by both children and adolescents.

Rule 4: "Women remember!" This rule is the shortest, but it's the most important. It is a rule that is often complained about by adolescent and adult males.

I would also like to leave you with the following anonymous Russian proverb: "Simply imagine that it's not your child, but someone else's. Everybody knows how to bring up other people's children."

Thank you for reading, and best wishes!

About the Author

Dr Aull is a behavioral pediatrician who has been diagnosing autism spectrum disorders and treating patients on the spectrum for more than 30 years. He practices in Carmel, Indiana, a suburb of Indianapolis, where he resides with his wife. Dr Aull spent 24 years in a general pediatric practice, which aided him in being able to distinguish normal behavior from abnormal behavior in children and young adults. For many years, Dr Aull has spoken at ADHD and autism conferences about the milder forms of autism spectrum disorders and how they may be diagnosed and treated.

Index

A

Abilify. *See* Aripaprazole (Abilify)

Abstraction of information, 73

Adderall. *See* Mixed amphetamine salts (Adderall)

ADHD
autism spectrum disorder, component of, 133
and dyslexia, 138–139
medications and suicidal ideation, 152–153
medications for. *See* Amphetamines; Methylphenidates; Nonstimulants; Stimulants
meltdowns, 140–141
stimulants exacerbating symptoms of, 186
subjects focused on, 151–152
treatment alone for Asperger's syndrome, 170

Aggression
atypical antipsychotics for, 38, 112, 114–116, 166
in low-functioning autism, 36

All Cats Have Asperger's Syndrome (Hoopman), 13

Function
    as classification of autism, 36
    IQ and, 36

G

Genetics
    male relatives, characteristics and occupations of, 22, 23
    mother's and her male relatives' characteristics, connection between, 23
Geodon. *See* Ziprasidone (Geodon)
Guanfacine (Intuniv), 159–160
    for ADHD, 159–160
    for sleep maintenance, 164

H

High-functioning Asperger's syndrome
    compared to low-functioning Asperger's syndrome, 44–45
    diagnosis of, 59
    driving, 48, 51
    employment and, 47–48
    family members also presenting with symptoms, 62–63
    flirting, 60

T

*Future Horizons is also proud to publish
these titles by Dr Temple Grandin*

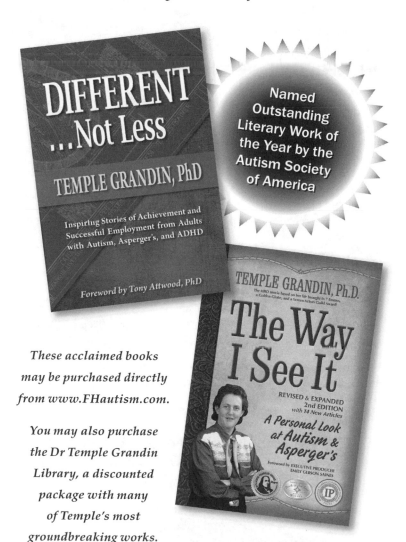

These acclaimed books
may be purchased directly
from www.FHautism.com.

You may also purchase
the Dr Temple Grandin
Library, a discounted
package with many
of Temple's most
groundbreaking works.

800•489•0727 | www.FHautism.com